BRIGHT NOTES

WAITING FOR GODOT, ENDGAME, AND OTHER WORKS BY SAMUEL BECKETT

Intelligent Education

Nashville, Tennessee

BRIGHT NOTES: Waiting for Godot, Endgame, and Other Works
www.BrightNotes.com

No part of this publication may be used or reproduced in any manner whatsoever without written permission, except in the case of brief quotations in critical articles and reviews. For permissions, contact Influence Publishers http://www.influencepublishers.com.

ISBN: 978-1-645423-84-3 (Paperback)
ISBN: 978-1-645423-85-0 (eBook)

Published in accordance with the U.S. Copyright Office Orphan Works and Mass Digitization report of the register of copyrights, June 2015.

Originally published by Monarch Press.
Walter James Miller; Bonnie E. Nelson, 1971
2020 Edition published by Influence Publishers.

Interior design by Lapiz Digital Services. Cover Design by Thinkpen Designs.

Printed in the United States of America.

Library of Congress Cataloging-in-Publication Data forthcoming.
Names: Intelligent Education
Title: BRIGHT NOTES: Waiting for Godot, Endgame, and Other Works
Subject: STU004000 STUDY AIDS / Book Notes

CONTENTS

1)	Introduction to Samuel Beckett	1
2)	Introduction to Beckett's Critical and Esthetic Position	25
3)	Waiting for Godot	32
4)	Waiting for Godot: Survey of Criticism	76
5)	Other Plays: Endgame	84
6)	Other Plays: Krapp's Last Tape	97
7)	Other Plays: All That Fall	101
8)	Three Novels: Molloy, Malone Dies, The Unnamable	103
9)	Essay Questions and Answers	110
10)	Bibliography	122

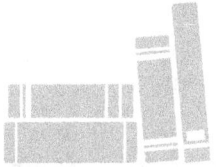

INTRODUCTION TO SAMUEL BECKETT

Samuel Beckett's importance is neatly summed up in the official statement made by the Swedish Academy when it awarded him the Nobel Prize for Literature in 1969:

> Beckett has exposed the misery of man in our time through new dramatic and literary forms. His ... muted minor tone holds liberation for the oppressed and comfort for the distressed.

It was characteristic of the gaunt, shy, baggy - suited Beckett ... who lives a life of almost monastic simplicity ... to announce that he would not go to Stockholm to accept his $80,000 prize in person. No one who knows Beckett well was surprised. His close friends tell us he is unable to stand praise or flattery of any kind. If he had attended the Nobel ceremonies, he would have been expected to wear formal clothes, make a formal speech, and talk about his work. But Beckett distrusts conformity and ceremony and, as we shall see, he doubts the validity of "public" language. Unlike many contemporary writers who are actively "engaged" in public life, Beckett prefers to address the world almost exclusively through his art. When he received the Prize money, it was reported that he gave most of it to "resistance" groups.

Some of Beckett's critics have assumed that he must have had a miserable childhood in order to write so much about the "misery of man." Beckett confounds these simple minds by stressing that he had a very happy childhood. He was born in 1906 near Dublin, where his father, a quantity surveyor, was a partner in the firm of Beckett and Metcalfe. The family was Protestant and solidly bourgeois; Samuel's mother and brother were both deeply religious. Young Samuel attended Earlsford House, a Protestant day school in Dublin, whose director, Monsieur Lepelon, planted in his protégé an interest in French culture. Later Samuel was sent to Portora Royal School (Oscar Wilde's school) at Enniskillen, County Fermanagh, in northern Ireland. This was a typical English Protestant "public" school which encouraged a life of rugged athletics and serious application to studies. Under the guidance of the French teacher, Mademoiselle Tennant, Beckett developed a lifelong passion for the Romance languages.

Back in Dublin in his late teens, Beckett frequented the Abbey Theatre, then featuring the works of J. M. Synge; and he attended Trinity College, where he majored in Italian and French, excelled in cricket and rugby, and earned a reputation as both a popular student and a non - conformist. For example, it was rumored that an essay of his was submitted to the examining professors on toilet paper. After Beckett took his B.A. in 1927, one of his teachers, Professor Rudmose Brown, arranged an exchange - lectureship for him at the École Normale Supérieure in Paris, where he taught for two years.

During this time he made the acquaintance of James Joyce, the Irish writer self - exiled in Paris whose novel *Ulysses* (1922) had established him as the master of stream - of - consciousness fiction. Joyce was engaged on a "Work in Progress." Beckett undertook a French version of parts of the "Work" and produced a brilliant exegesis of it, published as *Our Exagmination Round his Factification for Incamination of Work in Progress* (1929).

One day in 1930, Beckett heard that Nancy Cunard, Paris publisher, and Richard Aldington, poet and critic, were offering a prize of ten pounds for the best poem submitted on the subject of "Time." The deadline was next morning. Beckett swiftly composed a poem based on events in the life of the philosopher Rene Descartes, and rushed across Paris by night to make certain he got the manuscript into the publisher's mail - box before the deadline. "Whoroscope", as the poem was called, won the prize, was published by Miss Cunard's "The Hours Press" in a limited edition of 300 copies, and launched Beckett on his career as a creative writer.

In 1931 he returned to Trinity College as Lecturer in French and assistant to Professor Brown, earned his master's degree for research on Descartes, and published a probing, poetic essay on Proust. But in spite of his obvious talents as critic and scholar, Beckett came to feel unsuited for the academic life, and for the next four years he knocked around London and the Continent. His spiritual agonies during this period are reflected in his first volume of short stories, *More Pricks than Kicks* (1934), and especially in his volume of verse, *Echo's Bones and Other Precipitates* (1936).

In 1937, Beckett settled on Paris as his permanent home. Soon after, his father died, leaving the 32-year - old writer with a small inheritance on which he managed to eke out a sparse living until his plays achieved some financial success. One of his acquaintances of this period has described him as "dressed badly," with absolutely "no vanity about his appearance." He was tall, long - striding, with enormous green eyes "that never looked at you." He wore spectacles, seldom spoke, never said anything silly, and had a wonderful sense of humor.

Joyce was now suffering acutely from failing vision. All his friends, including Beckett, would help him by reading to him and by taking down passages of "Work in Progress" as Joyce dictated them. Beckett especially, with his subtle command of several tongues, was a great inspiration to Joyce who at that time was developing his techniques of multi - lingual punning. Beckett spent so much time in the Joyce household that the impression spread that he was "Joyce's secretary." Indeed, Joyce's daughter thought Beckett must actually be courting her. The young Irishman had to make it painfully clear he came mainly to see her father.

Joyce's "Work" was finally published in 1938 under the title of *Finnegans Wake*. And Beckett's technical debt to Joyce . . . as well as the ways his interests differed from those of the master . . . was made clear in Beckett's own first novel, *Murphy*, also published that year.

When World War II broke out in September 1939, Beckett, then in Ireland visiting his mother, returned to the Continent. "I preferred France in was to Ireland in peace," he later told *The New York Times*. After Paris fell, he joined a Resistance group. In August 1942, the group was discovered, several of his comrades were captured by the Nazis, and Beckett, fearing for his life, fled to the Vaucluse (Unoccupied Zone) and worked as a farm - hand near Avignon. In all the stress and confusion of war, he managed to work on his second novel, *Watt*. After the liberation of France, he served as interpreter and storekeeper with an Irish Red Cross unit at a field hospital at Saint Lo, was decorated for outstanding non - combat service, and married Suzanne, a girl he had met in the Resistance.

Settling down again in peacetime Paris, Beckett worked feverishly for five years in what he has since regarded as his greatest burst of creativity. Writing in French, he turned out his trilogy, *Molloy, Malone Meurt,* and *L'Innommable*; his first great play, *En Attendant Godot*; and a volume of stories and sketches, *Nouvelles et Textes pour Rien.* Later he produced English versions of each of these works: *Molloy, Malone Dies, The Unnamable*; *Waiting for Godot*; and *Stories and Texts for Nothing.*

Until his forty - seventh year, Beckett was well known only in literary and intellectual circles, and even then mainly as a translator and critic. But on January 5, 1953, *En Attendant Godot* was first performed in Paris. It was an instant critical and popular success, and ran for more than 300 nights. *Waiting for Godot* has since been translated into more than twenty languages, and is already considered a turning - point in modern drama.

For a long while, Beckett wrote nothing significantly new and indeed, thought he had run dry. Then in 1956 he completed *Fin de Partie.* Translating it into English, as *Endgame*, set him off on a new series of short works in his native tongue: *Krapp's Last Tape, Happy Days, Play,* and several radio and TV plays for the British Broadcasting Corporation. This second great burst of writing resolved itself in a free - verse novel, written first in French as Comment c'est (1961) and later in an English recreation, *How it is* (1964).

During the 1960's, Beckett became an influential figure in all dramatic media. In British television studios, in the streets of New York where he has done his film with Buster Keaton, in the "legitimate" theatre, he has worked firmly but easily with directors and actors, all of whom regard him as a natural genius. Lately he has served as his own producer. When not in rehearsal, he divides his time between his Paris house and his country cottage which he bought with the proceeds from *Godot*. He avoids the public eye. He gives few interviews, is rarely photographed, and indeed, after winning the Nobel Prize, went into virtual hiding for several months. News from his friends, however, indicated that the great multi - lingual artist was at work in a totally new world of imagination, on totally new forms, which John Calder described in 1970 as "more painterly than literary."

SAMUEL BECKETT: CHRONOLOGY

1906 April 13: Samuel Beckett is born at Foxrock, near Dublin, Ireland

1927 Graduates from Trinity College, Dublin, with B.A. in French and Italian

1928-1930 Reader in English in École Normale Supérieure, Paris

1930 Wins prize for poem "Whoroscope"

1930-1931 Lecturer in French, Trinity College

1931 Takes M.A., publishes essay on Proust

1932-1936 Wanders in England, France, Germany

1937 Settles permanently in Paris

1938 First novel, *Murphy*, published in London

1940 Paris falls to Nazis; Beckett joins Resistance

1942 Flees to Unoccupied Zone of France; writes *Watt*

1945 Joins staff of Irish Red Cross hospital at Saint Lo

1947 *Murphy* published in French

1947-1949 Writes trilogy of novels (*Molloy, Malone Meurt, L'Innommable*) and play En Attendant Godot

1951 *Molloy* and *Malone Meurt* published

1952 *En Attendant Godot* published

1953 January 5: premiere of *En Attendant Godot*, Paris *Watt* and *L'Innommable* published

1954 *Waiting for Godot* published in New York

1955 August: *Godot* plays in London *Molloy* published in New York *Nouvelles et Textes pour rien* published in France

1956 *Waiting for Godot* plays in Miami *Malone Dies* published in New York

1957 January 13: *All that Fall* produced by British Broadcasting Corporation *Fin de Partie* published in France April 3: *Fin de Partie* performed in French in London

1958 October 28: *Endgame* (in English) and *Krapp's Last Tape* open in London *Endgame* published in New York

1959 June 24: *Embers* broadcast by BBC

1961 *Comment c'est* published in France

September 17: *Happy Days* opens off - Broadway, New York

1962 November 13: *Words and Music* broadcast by BBC

1963 June 14: *Play* first performed, in German, at Ulm Cascando broadcast in Paris

1964 *Film* produced in New York with Buster Keaton *How it is* published in New York

1969 Beckett wins Nobel Prize for Literature

1970 *The Collected Works* published in New York

BECKETT'S PHILOSOPHICAL RELATIONS

Modern philosophy figures so prominently in Beckett's work that many critics find it convenient to treat him mainly in philosophical terms. Frederick Hoffman refers to the novels as "epistemological inquiries" and to the plays as "reflections upon the existence of God." Martin Esslin talks of Beckett's writings as the "culmination of existentialist thought," superior in some ways to the works of Sartre himself. And Jacquelin Hoefer plunges into a discussion of Beckett's *Watt* with the phrase, "In this philosophic **satire**, . . ."

Beckett himself . . . in both his poetry, fiction, and film - writing . . . makes many direct references to philosophers like Heraclitus, Descartes, Geulincx, Malebranche, and Berkeley. In all his creative writing, he freely uses concepts and images . . . sometimes details from the very lives . . . of these and other thinkers including St. Augustine and Wittgenstein. In interviews, he has been quoted as commenting on Heidegger and Sartre.

Obviously, then, there is considerable value in reviewing Beckett's philosophical relations ... direct and indirect, explicit or implicit ... with philosophers ancient and modern.

BECKETT AND HERACLITUS

An ancient Greek, Heraclitus (530-470 B.C.) typifies the bold thinker who accepts the evidence even when it shows him what he does not want to see. Heraclitus passionately hoped to find proof of permanence and unity in nature, but he had to admit that he could see only change and diversity. His famous example is that one cannot place the same foot in the same stream a second time ... neither the foot nor the stream is by then the same. "Everything flows" (including Heraclitus' tears, if the story of his disenchantment is accurate). To a modernist, Heraclitus stands for the beliefs that time is more real than space, that the many are closer to experience than the one, that becoming is closer to reality than being. A Beckett character would see Heraclitean flux not only in the outer world, he would experience it also in the inner world. Consciousness also fluctuates. One cannot contemplate that same foot, that same stream, twice with the same mind. For example, in Beckett's *How it is*, the narrator (who refers directly to Heraclitus: p. 34) qualifies his own account of his own existence by reminding us often that there have been many "states" in his life and many different "versions" of those states.

BECKETT AS A MODERN GORGIAS

An ancient Sicilian teacher, Gorgias of Lentini (483-375 B.C.), is supposed to have wrapped up this package of values: Nothing has any real existence; even if it did exist, it could not be known;

even if anything could be known, it could not be communicated. A. J. Leventhal has stressed that the last of these precepts implies that "it is impossible for any idea to be the same in different minds," and that this is the crux of the problem for Becketts' characters. And how could they express the inexpressible, anyhow? Precepts similar to Gorgias' basic assumptions become, as we shall see, central in Beckett's esthetics.

BECKETT AND SOCRATES

The teacher of Plato and the main character in the Dialogues, Socrates (467-399 B.C.) is reported to have said: "The unexamined life is not worth living." As Ruby Cohn points out, the Beckett hero goes further . . . he comes painfully to realize that even the examined life is not worth it, but still he must go on, analyzing himself, probing constantly into the nature of the Self and of Reality.

BECKETT AND AUGUSTINE

St. Augustine (345-430) was an early Christian theologian whose teachings are still influential today. One sentence in Augustine's writings especially fascinates Beckett. Referring to the two thieves who were crucified on either side of Jesus, Augustine says: "Do not despair, one of the thieves was saved; do not presume, one of the thieves was damned." Why did one thief earn grace, another perdition? This is the crux of the problem on Didi's mind at the opening of *Waiting for Godot*; *Molloy* in the first novel of the trilogy also thinks of the thieves. According to Alan Schneider, brilliant director of several Beckett productions, Beckett has observed that that Augustinian sentence has a "wonderful shape. It is the shape that matters." Shape matters:

form signifies. A Beckett character might feel, or suspect, that Augustine had really said that God is arbitrary. The Beckettian reader, accustomed to Beckettian ironies, would see in the very balance of the sentence a kind of psychological "iron law of wages" . . . man is given enough hope to keep him going, not enough to give him ideas.

BECKETT AND OCCAM'S RAZOR

William of Occam (1280-1349), an English monk, is famous for his Law of Parsimony, sometimes called "Occam's Razor" because it cuts to the bone. His Law states, in effect, that the burden of proof rests with the affirmative and that we must not multiply entities unnecessarily rigorously applied, his Law provides the basis for a scientific approach and for modern positivism. It is not necessary, for example, for a positivist to disprove the existence of an immortal soul or to reckon at all with the concept; rather it is incumbent upon the believer in the concept to prove it. This part of the Law already disabuses the positivist of much cumbersome lumber. The other proviso goes further: Occam would expect us to use the simplest explanation compatible with demonstrable truth. If a phenomenon can be explained in natural terms, there will be no need to go outside Nature to explain it. Again, if both the Ptolemaic and the Galilean approaches "work" in practical astronomy, the positivist would choose the Galilean system on the grounds of its greater simplicity alone.

Samuel Beckett applies something like Occam's Razor to his artistic problems. In his choice of settings, in his dramatization of human conduct and social problems, he cuts to the bone. His reason is Occam's: to keep the situation uncluttered with irrelevancies, in which the human mind often seeks refuge in its flight from the truth.

BECKETT'S PREOCCUPATION WITH DESCARTES

The "father of modern philosophy," Rene Descartes (1596-1650), founded his Cartesian system on deliberate doubt. The one fact he could not reasonably doubt was that he was doubting. To doubt is to think, and to think is to exist. Cogito ergo sum: I think, therefore I am. With similar methods of reasoning he arrived at the existence of God. The notion of a perfect being could not originate in the mind of an imperfect being because the imperfect cannot originate the perfect. Therefore the idea must come from a perfect Being. Therefore God exists: a perfect Being who cannot deceive.

Under God, Descartes postulated a sharply dualistic reality: there is matter, and there is mind (or soul). All matter is mechanical - the Universe is a mechanism, animals are automata, even the human body is a machine. But in addition to his body, man has a soul which, according to Descartes, is seated in the pineal gland in the center of the brain. The soul controls the body; and the soul understands the sciences, uses the "supervisory science" of mathematics to see the relationships among the sciences, and perceives the essential geometric nature of all motions and shapes.

Although Beckett is not a Cartesian, he may be called a "Descartes - intoxicated man." His poem "Whoroscope" purports to be a free - associational monologue by Descartes himself. And all Beckett's novels deal with heroes who are painfully aware of a sharp Cartesian dichotomy in their nature: their physical mechanism defects while their minds go on, their minds may lose control over their bodies, their minds may go out of commission while their bodies go on. Some critics see Beckett as sometimes dividing mind and body into two separate characters, for example, into Didi and Gogo, respectively, in *Waiting for Godot.*

As Hoffman makes clear, Beckett is especially obsessed with Cartesian considerations of man - as - machine and man - as - a - user - of - machines. If man is a machine created by a perfect Being, why is that machine so defective? If man can himself create machines, does he in some way resemble the Creator of man - as - machine? What are the responsibilities of a creator toward his defective creature, and vice versa, and of one creature toward another? As Hugh Kenner has pointed out, the bicycle figures prominently in many of Beckett's works: Beckett heroes - for example, Molloy - stand in a mind - body relation to their cycles, in a tableau that Kenner has brilliantly dubbed "the Cartesian Centaur." The perfect bicycle becomes a replacement for the imperfect body. And one of Descartes' own hypothetical machines is actually recreated by Beckett. In his *Discourse on Method*, Descartes says:

. . . for we may easily conceive of a machine to be so constructed that it emits vocables, and even that it emits some correspondent to the action upon it of external objects which cause a change in its organs; for example, if touched in a particular place it may demand what we wish to say to it; if in another may cry out that it is hurt, and such like . . .

We easily recognize this as the model for more than one situation in Beckett. In *How it is*, for example, the narrator's fist and can - opener are the "external objects" and poor Pim is the machine programmed to "emit vocables." When the narrator sees all humanity as thus paired off into sadists and masochists, he is thinking in effect that sadists are "men - as - users - of - machines" and masochists are "men - as - machines."

Again, in Beckett's fiction, most movements and shapes are described in Cartesian terms of lines, curves, squares, rectangles, polygons, parallelepipeds, circles, ellipses, triangles, and other geometric figures. All characters are obsessed with mathematical possibilities, formulations, combinations, permutations. In *Molloy*, a lame tramp tries to arrange in a complex series the pebbles he finds on the beach. In *Watt*, the main character wonders how many combinations of socks he can wear. In *Waiting for Godot*, as we shall see, it's a matter of calculating the "percentage," the spiritual odds.

Just as Descartes' cogito ergo sum led many of his successors to forsake a dualistic world of mind and body for a monistic world of mind only, so do Beckett's characters tend to become mainly thinking (therefore doubting) beings. The Beckett hero, we could say, far surpasses Descartes as a doubter: he certainly can doubt that he doubts, and he certainly can doubt that God cannot deceive. Several of these Beckett heroes are themselves writers, who in turn create new characters. What is the relationship of these characters to their creator, and their creator's relationship to Beckett? Such questions are in the air when a Beckett narrator suddenly suggests that maybe the story he is telling you is untrue. Maybe the new character he has told you about is simply another fantasized version of himself, or another fragment of his own divided self. This seems especially to be the case in the trilogy of novels.

A Beckett character, in short, is likely to feel not only that "I therefore I am," but also: "I think, therefore other selves exist," and "Others think, therefore I am." Such questions about man - the - perceiver and man - the - perceived occur to Didi, as we shall see, near the end of *Waiting for Godot*.

BECKETT AND OCCASIONALISM

Many of Descartes' successors could not accept his concept of the pineal gland, with its unlikely mechanism for gearing the soul to the body. But if you divide the human being into separable mind and body, how do they relate?

An alternative to Descartes' answer was offered by the Occasionalists, so called because they saw every interaction between mind and body as the occasion for divine intervention. Whenever the body is about to influence the soul, or the soul ready to direct the body, God himself determines the result. is no connection between body and soul within man himself. Most rigid of the Occasionalists was Nicole Malebranche (1618-1715), who denied any causality at all in nature; rather he saw every event as a manifestation of divine continuity: the Deity, through his interventions, literally recreates the Universe every second. Beckett's characters are often thinking of Malebranche and/or his doctrine. For example, when the narrator of *How it is* describes his own actions in opening a can, he sarcastically thinks of them as a series of little miracles, by which he must mean that whereas he himself willed each motion, God actually carried it out (p. 35). And so we must interpret a passage in which the narrator recalls a walk he took with a girl: the dog that was following them moved from place to place not because of them but because of repeated miracles. In this latter case, the narrator actually thinks of Malebranche by name (p. 30).

Beckett's favorite Occasionalist, though, is Arnold Geulincx (1624-1669) whose Ethics praised that man who seeks bliss in meditation instead of in overt action. In Beckett's short story "The End," the narrator explicitly refers to this book, which his tutor had given him (*Stories and Texts,* p. 63). Geulincx' maxim, "Where you are worth nothing, there you should want nothing," figures in Beckett's *Murphy*. And Geulincx' insistence that mind is powerful and free (indeed, God - like), but only in its own realm, resonates throughout the trilogy of novels: *Molloy* "loves" Geulincx, the Unnamable ponders him often.

The student of Beckett might ponder the relationship between Descartes, the Occasionalists, and *Waiting for Godot*. Didi and Gogo may agree to "go." But their bodies stand still. Descartes' "connection" has failed. Has Malebranche's God intervened? Have the tramps tried to extend the power of mind beyond its own realm?

BECKETT AND BERKELEY

George Berkeley (1685-1753) was an Irish philosopher who liked Descartes' cogito ergo sum (I think, therefore I am) but disliked Descartes' dualistic reality of mind and body. He resolved this by postulating that material things exist only because mind contemplates them. To the question of how the North Pole (then as yet unseen by man) could exist, Berkeley replied that God perceives it. Indeed, the common world exists as a totality only in God's mind. Berkeley's new monism is summed up in his motto Esse est percipi - to be is to be perceived. For this neat disposal of Descartes' dualism, Berkeley was awarded a bishopric.

Beckett is almost as much concerned with Berkeley's Esse est percipi as he is with Descartes' cogito ergo sum. In the middle of an apparently meaningless tirade, Lucky, the most abject character in *Waiting for Godot*, explicitly focuses our attention on Berkeley. And in the notes to the 1964 film script, Beckett explicitly amends Berkeley. Beckett says in effect that to be is to be perceived - by one's self! The kind of perception most important to man is self - perception: he does not really exist until he contemplates himself. But this takes great strength and courage. Dr. Carl Gustav Jung, post - Freudian psychoanalyst, declared that most people find nothing more painful than perceiving themselves. Yet without self -awareness, Jung tells us, no real unified Self is possible.

Most of Beckett's characters suffer interminably either from failure to face themselves or from the pain that results from only half - trying. In *Waiting for Godot,* Didi hovers on the verge of self - discovery but he is too terrified and so lapses into unfulfillment.

WITTGENSTEIN AND "WATT" - GENSTEIN

Ludwig Wittgenstein (1889-1951), a native Austrian who did much of his work in Great Britain, is both an influential and unique figure in modern philosophy. Influential, because his writings paved the way for Logical Positivism, one of the two most important philosophies in the West today. Unique, because he produced two highly original systems of thought, the second largely a rejection of the first! In his Tractatus Logico - Philosophicus (1922), Wittgenstein expounded seven propositions, some of which have found their way directly into recent fiction (e.g., Giles Goatboy). Most important for our purposes are: (1) The world is everything that is the case. (2) What is the case, the fact, is the existence of states of affairs; (3) a logical picture of facts is a thought; and (4) a thought is a sentence with a sense. Wittgenstein was coping with that dread problem in philosophy: how can you reason in language when you know language can be fallacious and ambiguous; when you do not know how language corresponds with reality?

The basis of Wittgenstein's first system is in that striking idea that a sentence is literally a picture. If it is a sentence with sense, then it shows its sense, simply by juxtaposing names of things in clear relationships; if the writer is precise in his naming, and if the reader or listener understands the names, then the relationships are comprehensible and unambiguous. However, Wittgenstein's last proposition is (7) Whereof one cannot speak, thereof one must be silent. In other words, Wittgenstein does conceive of a realm about which one can say nothing comprehensible. This may not mean much, however, since proposition (1) says that the world is all that matters.

At the end of *Tractatus*, Wittgenstein says:

My propositions are elucidatory in this way: he who understands me finally recognizes me as senseless, when he has climbed through them, on them, over them. (He must, so to speak, throw away the ladder, after he has climbed up on it.) He must surmount these propositions; then he sees the world rightly.

Thirty - one years later Wittgenstein published *Philosophical Investigations* which systematically refutes *Tractatus*. For example, the earlier work says that any new proposition can easily be anticipated because it would just be a new arrangement of names already known; but in the later work, Wittgenstein acknowledges that new life - situations of necessity lead to totally new names. Most important, though, is his new concept of the sentence. In *Tractatus*, a sentence means because it pictures; but in *Investigations,* the meaning of a sentence is in its use, its employment, its application.

At least one major historian of ideas believes that the *Tractatus* contains all the main theses of Logical Positivism. This school of thought insists on reasoning only from verifiable experience (which rules out **metaphysical** questions like immortality, separable soul, divinity) and tries to reduce language to propositions that reflect objective facts.

From *Murphy* (1938) to *How it is* (1961), Beckett characters are either caricatures of positivists or victims of a positivist culture. They are picayunely concerned with the accuracy of their everyday reasoning. They constantly try to verify even their own recent experience. They worry so much about precision of language that they almost erase themselves. Wittgenstein put all the talents of his later life into revising the major work of his early life. A typical Beckett character reduces this to the absurd. Every minute he puts all his energies into revising the previous minute.

Wittgenstein figures symbolically in *Murphy* and pervasively in *Watt*. When Murphy retires into his garret and pulls his ladder up after him, the action is symbolic: he has not thrown away the ladder, he has not really surmounted the situation. The author's own mysterious reference to "Louis" at this point becomes comprehensible when we realize that Louis is French for Ludwig: the reference is to Wittgenstein's ladder. In *Watt*, the main character might well be called Watt - genstein, so much is he a caricature. He is impelled to name everything; if he cannot name it, he takes ill. Like the author of *Tractatus*, Watt believes that everything new will be explainable in terms of names already known to him. Like a typical Logical Positivist, he seeks truth in external, sensory phenomena; what is not immediately accessible to the senses he tries to reason through with questions, hypotheses, mathematical arrangements and rearrangements of possibilities. A thorough rationalist, Watt believes that words and thought are identical; he never has to struggle with images, personal symbols, and inchoate notions before he delivers a sentence with a sense.

Wittgenstein saw the limits of such an approach ... especially with his proposition (7) . . . and he was in any event flexible enough to revise or even replace his system. But poor "Watt" - genstein is a mere technician of positivism; he is unable to tell when he has encountered something whereof one cannot speak!

When he is overwhelmed with unnamables, with complexities that will not submit to his grim logic-chopping, he disintegrates, he loses his mind, he talks gibberish.

The ladder motif figures here too. A minor character in *Watt* fell off a ladder when young; another makes an oblique reference to the ladder in language that echoes the ladder scene in *Murphy*; and of course, figuratively speaking, Watt has fallen off his ladder.

BECKETT AND EXISTENTIALISM

In a physical world of various particulars in constant flux, Descartes could see general mathematical truths that are fixed and immortal and to him, really the essence of things. And so there have always been thinkers prone to posit two levels of reality: a material, transitory, diverse, imperfect, subjective world, a world of becoming or existence; and an immutable, immaterial, perfect, objective world, a world of abstract ideas, of being or essence. These thinkers have seen the material world as related to man's senses, the world of ideas as related to his mind. Needless to say, to these philosophers, the abstract, mental world is the higher level; in Berkeley's case, the only real level. And to humanity at large, one net result has always been to set up a conflict between mind and body.

An influential modern philosopher, Soren Kierkegaard (1813-1855), re-examined these relationships. In his *Concluding Unscientific Postscript*, he decides that any abstract "truth" about the nature of the world, precisely because it has been abstracted from human experience, dies and becomes a mere "shell of truth." There can be no truth divorced from individual experience. Thus to Kierkegaard (as to Heraclitus), subjectivity is of a higher order than objectivity; becoming (existence) is prior to being (essence).

In other works (Either/Or; *The Concept of Dread*), Kierkegaard discusses the psychological effect on man of the fact that, through his intellect, he deals constantly with generalizations, abstractions, "essences." All the rest of his nature yearns for real experience, full expression, existence. This conflict of mind and heart leads to a crisis of despair. Man is paralyzed by dread (anguish, Angst). Of what? Why? Because if he breaks out of his mind - limited, objectivist way of life, the possibilities are infinite, and nothing is certain. Yet this period of dread is actually his one passageway to freedom.

In all crises, says Kierkegaard, man must act decisively. "The instant of choice is very serious, not so much on account of the rigorous cogitation involved in weighing alternatives, not on account of the multitude of thoughts related to every link in the chain, but because danger is abroad, danger that the very next instant it may not still be in my power to choose. It is important to choose . . . on time." For, as he tells us in his Journals, "The most tremendous thing which has been granted to man is the choice . . ." Thus Kierkegaard sees "intellect" and "cogitation" as serving man ill when they lead him to sterile abstraction, well when they help him to live action. Thought, to Kierkegaard, is thought only when it results in renewed existence.

Today's existentialism knows many variations. We can distinguish between "critical existentialists" who believe in crisis as the major force in growth, and "social existentialists" who believe that association, communion among people can also lead to maturation. There are religious existentialists like Karl Jaspers (1883-) and atheistic ones like Martin Heidegger (1889-) and Jean Paul Sartre (1905-). But whether they put their faith in personal "anguish" or social feeling, God or no God, they all agree that subjective existence precedes objective essence.

For example, Jaspers says: "We are Dasein, being there . . . man and only man produces languages, tools, ideas, acts . . . in short, he produces himself." Sartre says that whether God exists or not is irrelevant; man to be manly must act as if there is no God. He must not look outside himself for excuses, justification, guidance, salvation: "We are alone." "I choose myself, not in my being, but in my manner of being . . . I ought to know that if I do not choose, I am still choosing . . ."

Whether they know it or not, most of Beckett's characters are caught in an existentialist crisis of despair. His first fictional hero is Belacqua Shuah, **protagonist** of the short stories in More Pricks than Kicks. Belacqua is based on a character in Dante's Purgatory (Canto iv) who assumes a foetal position, head on knees, waiting apathetically in death as he had in life. In Beckett's modern version, Belacqua never really commits himself, he drifts into relationships without real "choice," he postpones every decision until it seems to come from without. *Waiting for Godot*, as we shall see, can be considered the central work in Beckett's exploration of the existentialist crisis. The main characters yearn vaguely for existence, yet they insist on looking outside themselves for salvation. Up against the need to choose, they choose by failing to choose.

BECKETT'S OWN POSITION IN PHILOSOPHY

Some critics are fond of saying that while he was writing his original versions in English (until he finished *Watt*), Beckett focused mainly on positivism, and that once he began composing his first versions in French (the trilogy; *Godot*), Beckett shifted his main concern to existentialism. This is too pat and can lead to oversimplification about both periods. For example, Beckett's *Proust*, published in English in 1931 long before any of the major works were written, is largely existentialist in its sympathies. And *Watt* itself, while it is a **satire** on positivism, is a satire with an existentialist message: Watt tries to live by mind alone, the rest of his nature rebels, his mind does not survive the existential crisis. Furthermore, in 1961 Beckett published, in English, *Happy Days*, concerned in part with existentialist concepts, and also published, in French, *How it is*, which satirizes both existentialism and positivism.

In any event, so far as Beckett's own philosophy is concerned, it is less valuable to think of Positivism and Existentialism as polar opposites and more constructive to think of what these two contemporary modes of thought have in common. Both see the search for Truth as a never - ending project; both see philosophy's task not as the promulgation of final doctrine but rather as the development of methods, attitudes, techniques. Both, in short, are more concerned with means than with ends. And both insist on finding the answers by human means; both say in effect that the question of God is irrelevant. While positivism takes objectivity as its starting point, and existentialism takes subjectivity, they agree in practice that man must be the measure of all things. In all the ways in which these two modes resemble each other, Beckett seems to agree with both of them.

We can sum up this discussion of Beckett's philosophical relations with these main points:

1. Beckett is artistically interested in the psychological effect a system of philosophy can have on people. How does a certain system of values help or hinder a person? How does it color his view of the world? of himself?

What happens if he comprehends only part of the system? Does a man choose the philosophy that suits his temperament?

2. In his artistic methods and emphases, Beckett reflects a subjectivist orientation in philosophy. While he obviously sees the subjective realm as the starting point of all inquiry about man's condition, he cannot be classified strictly in any school. He comes closest to being an existentialist, but there are criticisms of existentialism implicit in his later works.

3. Beckett is also indebted to philosophy for its aid to the artist in identifying the nature of the crucial questions for our time. As posed implicitly by Beckett himself, these include: What is Man? Is he entirely or partly a machine? Why does he regard himself as divided into warring parts (mind - body, rational - irrational, active - passive, conscious - unconscious, past - present, etc.)? Are these dichotomies real and inevitable? If real, how can he live with them constructively? If unreal, how can he rediscover self - unity? How can he perceive himself without becoming paralyzed by self - consciousness? What is Man's proper relation to outer reality? How can he discover that relation? How can he be certain of his discoveries? If he cannot achieve certainty, how can he live without it? How can he (in the face of all these paralyzing questions, and without recourse to self - deception) survive?

INTRODUCTION TO BECKETT'S CRITICAL AND ESTHETIC POSITION

Beckett scrupulously avoids commenting on his own works. He obviously feels that the works must speak for themselves, that they must mean what they will mean for the reader. But he has written criticism of other writers; he has published a series of three dialogues on the problem of the contemporary artist; and he has, on one occasion at least, been successfully interviewed about the general problem of today's writer. (On that occasion, absolutely in character, he identified the "key word" in his plays as: perhaps.) From these sources we can construct a notion of Beckett's critical and esthetic position as he himself has perceived it.

BECKETT ON JOYCE

In 1929, young Beckett published *Our Exagmination Round his Factification for Incamination of Work in Progress*. This was an exegesis of James Joyce's masterpiece, then known as a work in progress and later finished under the title of *Finnegans Wake*. In this massive novel about the unconscious mind, Joyce uses Jung's theory of the collective unconscious: each person's unconscious contains suppressed memories not only from his own experience but also from the experience of the whole human race. These memories flow through the mind of the sleeping **protagonist**, H. C. Earwicker (*Here Comes Everybody*), who in this state exists as every male from Adam and Noah down to Romeo, Darwin, Huck Finn and even Earwicker himself.

In the very title of his critique . . . with its portmanteau word exagmination (exaggeration as well as examination) . . . Beckett proclaims himself a lover of Joycean language techniques. In the essay proper, he makes productive comparisons between Joyce and Dante, partly in terms of "Cartesian" forms. Dante's *Inferno* he characterizes as "static lifelessness" of absolute malice; the *Paradise* as "static lifelessness" of absolute virtue. In between, he finds dynamic art: *Purgatory* is flowing with vitality. And Beckett sees "Work in Progress" as set entirely on the purgatorial level, containing all the tensions between good and evil, male and female, mind and body, objectivity and subjectivity, all the polarizing opposites. Joyce's "Work" is characterized by its "absolute absence of the Absolute." In form, Beckett sees Dante's *Purgatory* as conical: its shape implies progression upward, toward Paradise, toward absolute, static perfection. But Joyce's purgatory is spherical: its shape implies movement around, curving forward and backward toward cyclical repetition, in constant flux. Such observations reveal that even in his early twenties, Beckett emphasized one characteristic of great art: its complex material can be contained in a simple form faithful to the **theme**. Beckett as artist later lives up to the formal expectations of Beckett the critic.

BECKETT ON PROUST

Two years later, Beckett published his essay on Marcel Proust (1871-1922), author of *Remembrance of Things Past*, a seven -

volume psychological novel about decadent French aristocrats. Early in this pioneering work, Proust's hero discovers that he can evoke the very quality of past experience by simply yielding to the undertow of free association. Henceforth he lives subjectively on three levels of "sensation": recollection, immediacy, anticipation. The present becomes for him mainly a stage for past and future.

In his critique, Beckett focuses on Proust's view of the Self and on his method of analyzing that Self. The Proustian hero is seen struggling to assemble an identity from different periods, and different levels, of his own history. Beckett fastens significantly on the problem of habit versus spontaneity. It is here that he uses his well - known **metaphor** describing the individual as the seat of a continuous process of "decantation," a pouring from one vessel of clear fluid of the future into a second vessel of "agitated" fluid of the past. Beckett emphasizes that Proust presents phenomena in non - logical fashion, just in the order in which they are perceived subjectively. In effect, Beckett here rejects both the conventional plot, which rearranges life into neat patterns to make interesting reading and to "prove" a moral point, and Zola's "scientific" novel, which purports to present life - data in absolute fidelity to objective cause and effect. Beckett recalls Schopenhauer's definition of artistic method as a viewing of the world independently of the "principle of reason."

In this essay we see the origins of some important questions for Beckett to tackle in his own work later. How can the stultifying effect of habit be adequately represented on stage and page? How can fragmented man piece together an ego without peering so much into that murky fluid of the past?

BECKETT ON DEVLIN

In 1938, Beckett wrote an article for *Transition* magazine defending the work of Denis Devlin, whose poetry had been attacked for "obscurity." Beckett said in so many words that art has nothing to do with clarity. Other remarks in the review imply that even though the artist must risk being difficult if not downright solipsistic, there is still hope that art can achieve honest expression. The kind of thing Beckett had in mind can best be considered in connection with a major critical work written a decade later.

BECKETT ON MODERN PAINTERS

In 1949 Beckett and Georges Duthuit published "Three Dialogues" in which, ostensibly, they argue about works by Tal Coat, Masson, and Bram Van Velde. (These dialogues also appeared in *Transition* and have been reprinted in Esslin's valuable anthology; see Further Reading.) In the first dialogue, Beckett hopes for an art that will honestly admit that the artist's problem now is this: - there is really nothing to express, nothing with which to express it, and yet there remains an obligation, a compulsion to express it. In the last dialogue, Beckett takes the stand that Van Velde is the first to produce an art that freely acknowledges that "to be an artist is to fail, as no other dare fail ... that failure is his world."

In these *Transition* pieces, we must see Beckett as attacking the smug, facile, simplistic clarity achieved by popular artists and demanded by popular critics. If the artist is to tell the truth, he must begin ... as Gorgias of Lentini began (see p. 15) ... by admitting that we know nothing and that we do not even possess proper means with which to express that ignorance.

This nothing, this zero, can still be used as a starting point if we give up pseudo - clarity and strike out anew for honest art that contemplates problems instead of manufacturing quick, reassuring answers.

But "nothing" as Beckett uses the word here could also mean Kierkegaard's nothing which man faces in his crisis of despair. Before he can break out of his trap, he has to admit that the possibilities then would be infinite and nothing would be certain. Only by being willing to face the possibility of nothingness can man find Existence. But no matter how we interpret these key words in these four *Transition* pieces, they add up to mean that we must suffer the creative anxiety of plunging into the unknown.

BECKETT AND SCHNEIDER

In 1958, Alan Schneider, brilliant director of many stage and film productions of Beckett's work, published some of his correspondence with "Sam" in the *Village Voice* and a "personal chronicle" of their collaborations in *Chelsea Review*. (These two periodicals are a must for anyone who wants wholly to experience Beckett's world.) The letters reveal again that Beckett is determined to let his works speak for themselves and to let the "responsibility" for interpretation be the interpreter's. Here is one clear answer to the question often posed in Beckett's work, as we have suggested in our discussion of his philosophical relations: What is the relation between Creator and creature? They are both on their own, once the act of creation is completed. In the "chronicle," Schneider gives us a clear idea of one of the senses in which Beckett has used the word "failure" in his critical writing. He reports that Beckett has told him that failure in the popular sense is something he has breathed in all his life. Putting this together with the *Devlin Review*, we can see that Beckett means he is incapable of clarity in the popular sense; to be a real artist is to fail "as no other dare fail." (Again, the student interested in Beckett should follow closely the stage and film creations of Schneider.)

THE DRIVER INTERVIEW

In 1960, Tom F. Driver, one of our most profound students of drama, interviewed Beckett "by the Madeleine" in Paris; he published an account of the conversation in *Columbia University Forum*, and later used material from it in his 1970 treatise, *Romantic Quest and Modern Query*. (The original piece is reprinted in full in the *Stanley Clayes* anthology: see Further Reading.) In this conversation, Beckett emphasized the distress, the chaos, the mess in the world today. "The one chance of renovation," he said, "is to open our eyes and see the mess." It is not a chaos the artist created, and it's not a mess we can easily "make sense of." Nevertheless, "to find a form that accommodates the mess, that is the task of the artist now."

CONCLUSION: BECKETT'S ESTHETIC POSITION

When we consider these critical statements in the context of Beckett's artistic creations, we can formulate a consistent Beckettian esthetic. Modern man is paralyzed with confusion in both his inner and outer worlds. His personality is fragmented; his consciousness is at odds with itself and in constant flux. He cannot be certain of his perceptions or even express those perceptions in a way that will be reliably communicated. How can he function as a unified Self? The outer world, shorn of absolutes, cut loose from heaven above and hell below, is in a state of even greater chaos. What is the relation between the outer purgatory and the inner purgatory? Conventional art is adding to the "mess" by using forms and techniques that deny the existence of the mess. Conventional criticism adds to the confusion by demanding a clarity that isn't there. For example, the "clear," well - knit plot of traditional drama and fiction is a distortion of life; traditional literature puts great faith in beautiful language, as though language corresponds to reality; and the traditional artist strives to give his art the illusion of life, to seduce his audience into a "willing suspension of disbelief," which may no longer be a useful approach. Obfuscation parades as clarity.

In this crisis, we must find new forms, new approaches that help us to open our eyes and keep them open. We must not be like the narrator of *How it is* who opens his eyes briefly, glimpses the truth, and shuts them quickly (p. 94), or like Didi in *Waiting for Godot* who comes within a sniff of the truth and shies away (pp. 58-58a). Notice that Beckett, often accused of being a nihilist, speaks of the task of the artist now.

For the conventional mind, Beckett's work is made doubly painful. Beckett devises forms that make views of the mess almost unavoidable. And he is committed to an intensely subjectivist approach. He starts always from the assumption that men are because they think. But Beckett's characters do not think very often in well - packaged Cartesian or Wittgensteinian sentences. Instead, they think in a flow of images, in a struggling **syntax** conceived not by logical positivism but by existential agony.

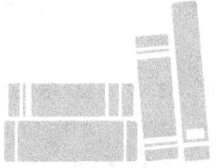

WAITING FOR GODOT

HISTORY OF THE PLAY

En Attendant Godot was composed between 1947 and 1949 when Beckett was experiencing his first of two great sustained bursts of radical originality. The French version was published in 1952 and opened in Paris on January 5, 1953, for a run of more than 300 performances. The English version was published in New York in 1954, played in London the following year, and had its American premiere at Cocoanut Grove, Florida, on January 3, 1956. Bert Lahr, star of the Florida presentation, played Gogo again when the show moved to New York on April 19, with E. G. Marshall as Didi, Kurt Kasznar as Pozzo, and Alvin Epstein as Lucky. These also were the principals (with Luchino Solito De Solis as the boy - messenger) for the Columbia Masterworks recording produced the same year. Since then the play has been performed in twenty tongues ... in such scattered parts of the world as Japan, Sweden, Yugoslavia ... and in all types of theatre: on campus, in summer stock, in "little theatres," and in prisons.

CONTROVERSIAL RECEPTION

Almost every opening night of *Godot* has been marked by extreme reactions. The Paris production was hailed by many critics as a major breakthrough in the drive toward a new drama. At the San Quentin Prison presentation, the inmates responded as never before to a theatrical piece. But in Miami, a large segment of the audience left in disgust before the curtain rose for act two. And after seeing the London production, a distinguished American critic heaped ridicule on Beckett, referring, for example, to two of his characters as "symbolic maniacs." "Nothing happens," other critics complained. "Nihilism," others said, as though that would make the play itself disappear. "There is no development," some discerned, meaning either that no problem is posed and solved, or that no character "grows," or both. The play was just a bundle of paradoxes and non sequiturs to the champions of clarity, cause - and - effect, and "significance" in art.

Many a critic who found the work beneath contempt enjoyed proving that "nothing happens" by giving a terse summary of the (in)action . . . terse enough to demonstrate that the second act is pretty much the same as the first. Like Didi himself, many of the critics came closer to sensing the truth than they realized, and then shied away just as fast.

Is it true that nothing happens in *Godot*? Why should the form as well as the content of the play have aroused such controversy? Why does the audience experience no "resolution," no "catharsis," in the usual sense of these terms? Why should so many distinguished critics have been caught off base? Why was it impossible for Beckett to say what he had to say in a more conventional form, with a more conventional approach? What clues does the play itself give us as to why it would . . . for some playgoers, at least . . . inevitably fail?

To probe these questions meaningfully, we should remind ourselves of the precise order in which the most important events actually take place in the play. (Where it seems advisable for the student especially to review the text in detail, we shall give the pertinent page numbers from the Evergreen (E-33) paperback edition.)

WHAT ACTUALLY HAPPENS IN GODOT?

Near a bare, roadside tree, two tramps meet as they meet daily: to wait for Godot. Estragon ("Gogo") fusses with his boots, Vladimir ("Didi") with his hat; Gogo naps but cannot recount his dreams because Didi won't listen; they discuss separation (but make up), suicide (but defer it), vegetables, religion, Didi's urinary troubles, and Godot. Passing through are Pozzo (with a whip) and his serf Lucky (on a leash, carrying Pozzo's coat, etc.). Pozzo, who owns the surrounding terrain, introduces himself, smokes, champions clock - time, discusses selling the serf, his ex - teacher; Lucky weeps but rewards Gogo's proffer of a handkerchief with a kick. On command, Lucky dances and "thinks." Master and slave resume traveling. A goat - boy brings a message: Godot will come tomorrow. Didi questions him about his brother, a shepherd. Night falls. Gogo sets his boots on the road for some passerby. Agreeing to leave, the tramps stand still. Next day, the tree has five leaves. The tramps resume waiting with games, calisthenics, philosophical talk. Didi finds and wears Lucky's hat; Gogo finds boots apparently left in exchange for his. Pozzo (now blind) and Lucky (now mute) return and collapse. The tramps deliberate over whether to help; they fall too, but finally help Pozzo up. Pozzo, disparaging clock - time, goads Lucky into traveling. Didi soliloquizes on his predicament. The boy brings the same message. Didi questions him about Godot. Night falls. The tramps plan to return tomorrow. Agreeing to leave, they stand still.

SOME CRUCIAL QUESTIONS ABOUT THE ACTION

Why is the play set in such a sparse "Nowhere"? Who is Godot? Why should anyone wait for him? Why should he send a messenger? Why do these incompatible tramps spend so much time together? Why are they separated by night and reunited by day? What really do all these chats on philosophical matters and clock - time add up to? What are the boots, hats, leash, and tree intended to symbolize? Why is the action broken up into so many disconnected little "routines," skits, and bits? Why do the tramps always agree to go, and then stand there? What does the action itself add up to? A detailed exploration of these questions should make it clear why *Waiting for Godot* is a landmark in dramatic history and why its author was awarded the Nobel Prize.

SIGNIFICANCE OF THE SPECTACLE IN WAITING FOR GODOT

The setting and props remind us of Gorgias' caution that nothing really exists and Occam's precept that entities must not be multiplied unnecessarily. Beckett's sparse "Nowhere" is our first clue to his reductive technique. He is intent on reducing his materials to the inescapable essentials, down close to a starting point of zero.

MEANING OF THE SETTING

The stark stage set forces us to concentrate on space and time. Possibility of "Cartesian" motion through space is indicated by the road. Possibilities of changes with time are indicated by the tree.

Later, if we're not too impatient with the playwright for taxing our perceptive power, we might come to associate the road with Pozzo and Lucky whom we recognize as the active ones; they go places, they're "on the road," always on the go. And we might even see religious allusions, for example to the Road to Emmaus (Gospel according to Luke, chapter 24). We will associate the tree with Gogo and Didi, not only because that's where they always meet but because a tree symbolizes the things Gogo and Didi are, do, and think about. Like a tree, Gogo and Didi vegetate, and indeed, the foods they most often discuss are vegetables. And the Tree, like the Road, has fundamental religious significance. Adam and Eve were forbidden to eat of the Tree of Knowledge of Good and Evil. They did. That may be one of the reasons why Didi and Gogo are here contemplating the nature and fate of man. This single tree constitutes their private Garden of Eden. Also, Jesus was crucified on crossed tree - beams (p. 34a) and so were the two thieves (pp. 8a-9a). And Judas hanged himself from a tree. When, as we have seen, the tree sprouts a grand total of five leaves, it obviously indicates the arrival of Spring. But the main point here is the sparseness of the foliage: for modern man, the set indicates, there is relatively little difference between dead Winter and blooming Spring. In the theatre, many spectators have to have it pointed out to them that the leaves have sprouted, so minuscule is the addition. Even the lighting is used for basic symbolic purposes. Notice that after the goat -boy brings his message that Godot will not come today, that is when night falls. Light, in other words, is hope; in some of Beckett's works (e.g., *How it is*), continuous light is grace. Darkness is hopelessness, despair, damnation.

MEANING OF THE PROPS AND COSTUMES

Just as he reduces the setting to the most significant essentials, so Beckett employs only the most meaningful of props. The leash that Lucky is "on" obviously symbolizes his bondage, his belonging to an owner. But again there is a deeper meaning. The man holding the leash is also considerably limited by this connection. There is symbolism too in the boots and hats. Gogo fusses with footwear because he is concerned not only with "body" but also with his roots in the earth; Didi fusses with headwear because he feels more related to "mind," the rational side of life. Every bit of costume is equally significant. The costume of a tramp is ill - fitting and second - hand, and his interest in trading and acquiring different clothing is an interest in trying out new identities in a search for his own. Pozzo's costume emphasizes his "higher" social status in two ways: his coat is carried by a slave acting as a valet; and in most productions of *Godot* . . . as we can see even in the pictures on the Columbia Masterworks album . . . Pozzo is "made up" to look like a brazen idol.

PANTOMIME AND "ROUTINE"

Beckett achieves some of his finest dramatic effects through frequent use of pantomime and circus - like or vaudeville - like "routines." These serve perfectly his "Proustian" concern with habit and his "Cartesian" concern with man - as - a - machine and man - as - a - user - of - machine. He has, on occasion, written an entire play in the form of a mime (e.g., Act without Words); directors casting for a Beckett play are on the lookout for actors with mime experience; and it is important to note that Beckett's Film stars Buster Keaton, genius of the silent - film era. In *Waiting for Godot,* one of the most important bits of "business" is the fall of all four main characters into a pitiful heap; some of them are there because they had delusions of grandeur about how they could help the ones who had collapsed first. Never has the so - called "low comedy" technique of deflation of human vanity been used to such poignant artistic ends. These four have touched bottom, the pantomime says; they have reached their fulfillment as men. And when the tramps do their "calisthenics," this routine symbolizes all the meaningless make - work that mankind has endured hour by hour while waiting for salvation. (Consider, for example, the discussion of make - work in Richard Dana's *Two Years before the Mast*.) And where we see the most powerful use of routine movement is in Pozzo's use of Lucky as a virtual automaton, man - as - a - machine programmed with habits that serve man - as user - of - machines.

BECKETT AND "TOTAL THEATRE"

Spectacle, then, is extremely important in Beckett. This has not always been the case with modern dramatists. Usually their language carries the greatest burden of the meaning; the theatre has been "literary" in its emphasis. Dialogue, speech, verbal poetry have been supreme. In a culture that has equated intellect with language, spectacle has been regarded as vulgar. Consider, for example, the critical reaction to that scene in J. M. Synge's *Riders to the Sea* in which neighbors carry into the cottage a dripping canvas sail containing a drowned body. Some reviewers called this a cheap, sensational "trick." But Beckett, who saw Synge's plays while at college in Dublin, goes further than Synge in the use of visual effects. In Synge, spectacle is still largely an illustration, a reinforcement of the language. In Beckett, spectacle "says" many things on its own, things essential to the total meaning and not said initially any other way. In this sense Beckett is closely related to those cinematic playwrights, like Alain Robbe - Grillet and Paddy Chayefsky, whose work from its very inception is developed in audio - visual terms. Beckett is probably the first great English writer to compose plays so thoroughly in terms of "total theatre."

SIGNIFICANCE OF THE STRUCTURE IN WAITING FOR GODOT

We have said that the form of *Godot* has meaning both in itself and in the way it differs from traditional dramatic form. For full appreciation of *Godot*, then, we should remind ourselves of what we mean by the **conventions** of dramatic structure.

TRADITIONAL FORM

Analysts of drama, from Aristotle (384-322 B.C.) down to Gustav Freytag (1816-1895) and Lajos Egri (1886-1967), have developed a well - respected set of precepts about how a play should open, develop, and conclude. They are well - respected largely because they reliably produce "successful" plays for the commercial theatre. According to this standard formula, the playwright supposedly should contrive to introduce his characters and their background as quickly as possible because they . . . and he . . . must focus on a problem. He must then propel his main characters into a conflict over that problem. By ingenious plotting . . . or arrangement of the order of events, confrontations, revelations . . . the playwright leads his characters to a crisis, a turning point so decisive that hereafter their lives will never be the same. If the playwright contrives a credible success for his characters, we have a happy ending, a comedy. If he leads them to a credible failure, we have a tragedy. In either event, we in the audience supposedly have experienced catharsis: that is, we have become emotionally involved and then we have been purged of these emotions (e.g., pity, terror) by developments that we understand and accept as "inevitable" and "just." We have experienced insights into the nature of man, we leave the theatre supposedly satisfied that man's condition can be explained.

DECLINE OF THE TRADITIONAL PLOT

Why should so many modern playwrights look askant at this traditional formula? In the first place, it is related to that mode of thought that strives for transcendent, absolute truth, for insight into the essence of a situation as separated from the human experience of it. This plot outline itself is an abstract design . . . abstracted or generalized from successful dramas of the past. And it is based on, and tends to confirm, the belief that there is a coherent "story" or reasonable explanation behind all events, not only in one man's life but in all history. According to this traditional view, life has meaning, purpose, direction, focus, essence. But the avant - garde thinker, uncertain of our perception of even the most immediate reality, is even more distrustful of abstract reality, especially if it is based on generalizations from past experience. He strongly doubts the validity of traditional notions of cause - and - effect, especially in judging human conduct. Since he cannot know the ultimate consequences of any human act, he doubts that any event can be regarded at the time of its occurrence as intrinsically good or evil. How, then, can we design a coherent plot?

"I distrust all people whose stories hang together," says a typical anti - hero in Ernest Hemingway's *The Sun Also Rises*. The avant - garde writer suspects that "story" has been imposed on facts, after the facts, and that the story inevitably re - shapes the facts. Of course, he doubts even more that "history" happened that way. Rather he sees "history" as the historian's own reconstruction of the past. The "beginning, middle, end" that historians, dramatists, novelists are found of seeing in their materials is their creation, subjective not at all objective in nature. One simple example will suffice. For centuries, all history was written (and past history re - written) to conform to the Christian interpretation of man's place and future in the scheme of things: the beginning in Divine

Creation, the crisis in the Crucifixion, the resolution in man's attainment of Heaven. As Tom F. Driver, professor of theology and drama, has pointed out, this "master - plot" of history has lost its authority for modern man.

"Beckett," Driver says, "has made many aware that it was not just this particular plot that was waning in power but also the very notion of any plot as a model for the interpretation of human existence."

STRUCTURE OF GODOT

And so we can see one reason why Beckett outraged the conventional expectations of the Establishment. "A Tragicomedy in Two Acts" would be expected to rise to a crisis, somewhere at or after the end of Act I, and to descend thereafter to a meaningful resolution, a **denouement**, in Act II. Freytag would even have diagrammed it as follows:

But what is the shape of *Godot?* We can see it if we outline Act I as follows:

The "Passive" Ones Pass The Time Waiting

The "Active" Ones Pass Through

The "Passive" Ones Get The Message

The "Passive" Ones Decide To Go On Waiting

Then notice that Act II could be outlined with exactly the same four headings! The beginning is in the end, the end is in the beginning; neither is either.

The action of Act I describes a circle, and the structure of Act II is another circle. Moreover, the clear implication is that every day's action in the past has been cyclical and every future day will go round - and - round too. As our summary of the action has shown, many of the separate little "bits" also go round in circles. The tramps may discuss breaking up their relationship, or killing themselves, or going off together, but every such discussion brings them right back around to their ambivalent beginning.

There is one major difference between Acts I and II. True, both acts conclude where they started, so far as the passive ones are concerned. But things seem different for the active ones. In Act II, Pozzo has lost his sight and has changed his views on the validity of clock - time; Lucky has lost his power of speech; both stagger and fall. Their condition now is nearer to that of the broken - down and penniless tramps. We do not know the causes of these effects: they seem simply to be in the course of things. And what will Lucky and Pozzo be next time around? All we know for certain is that they are spiraling down.

SOURCE OF TENSION

How does such a play . . . with no sharply drawn conflict; no inexorable movement; no converging of all awareness toward a peak of agony; no triggered release, no programmed catharsis . . . how can such a play still achieve dramatic tension? We do have the simple unique suspense of seeing what two people up against Nothing will do next. While we have no building up of sharp anxiety, we do have a renewal of interest in each of a series of pathetic efforts. And while there is no insistent overpowering undertow, there is the pervasive odor of an appalling question: Who is Godot that anyone should spend time waiting for him? Beyond that, there is no pistoned mechanism for the manufacture of dramatic tension. There is, however, a new kind of catharsis in store for the audience, as we shall see later in our discussion.

THE MESSAGE OF THE FORM

Let us sum up, then, the message of *Godot* as it is suggested in the structure of the play. At the bottom, life is cyclical; above that, it is spiraling downward; in either case, life seems repetitious, empty, boring, with no meaning in the sense of "purpose" or "progress." The passive ones know this and show it most clearly. The active ones succeed in ignoring it for a time, and they seem meanwhile to be "getting places," but they are gradually slowed down into realizing that motion is the merest illusion of action: that Life, one way or the other, is Closure. Perhaps for that reason the passive ones are closer to whatever truth there may be. Maybe, as we shall see in our analysis of the characters, the passive ones might even be closer to a way out of the spiral trap.

THE MEANING OF CHARACTERIZATION

In *Godot,* Beckett has produced characters whose names have become by - words on the cultural scene. They have become master symbols for forces in the modern personality. Two of them already rank among the most discussed and maybe even most beloved characters in all of dramatic literature.

TRADITIONAL CHARACTERIZATION AND THE AVANT - GARDE

Again, Beckett accomplished this while ignoring all the critical criteria that had reached the status of immutable truths in the

Establishment. Traditionally, characterization had come to mean the positivistic exposure of a believable personality to significant events that would challenge him to transcend himself: both the events and his interaction with them are supposed to be credibly motivated. From his experience, his fate, we are supposed to achieve some understanding of the causes and effects of man's condition. In other words, Freytag's diagram of the structure of a play should also serve as a chart of the excitement the hero experiences in a critical period of his life.

But such a neatly organized package, as we have seen, is distrusted by the avant-garde who suspect that the contents are created to fill out the container. In any event, Freytag's drama is designed to explain the "realistic world," the "objective world," in that world's own smug terms. Beckett is more interested in studying mankind from entirely new perspectives. Thus Freytag and Aristotle have no relevance for *Waiting for Godot*. Notice that the main characters hardly change in the "dramatic" sense of the word "change." The other two principal characters change drastically but without any clear "motivation" in the traditional sense. Again, there are indications that two or maybe all four of the principal characters are not even distinct, separate personalities but rather parts of a divided self. The only way to judge them, to discuss them, is the way Beckett created them . . . without any reference to the usual criteria or even to the "realistic" world. In other words, to use a favorite existentialist phrase, let us look at these characters as they are . . . there.

ESTRAGON

Of the two tramps, Gogo impresses us as the earthier one. He seems to be more animal, more related to things physical. His concern with his boots symbolizes concern with his roots in the soil. He seems to be in easy communion with the "darker side" of human nature. He strikes us as unafraid of the instinctive, irrational, unconscious forces in himself. Comparing Gogo's and Didi's reactions to a new situation, we might observe that Gogo responds almost instinctively to the implicit quality of the occasion, while Didi is more likely to judge it on its verbal, explicit merits. Just as Gogo accepts himself more readily, so does he come to terms with the social world as it is. This is not to say that Gogo is unintellectual, by any means. He impresses us as being cultured; he uses a magnificent vocabulary with great casualness. But he seems to have little faith in abstract reasoning on any question, no matter how brilliantly he may comment on it. (See pp. 9A, 39, 48A, 53A.) His subjectivity, skepticism, resignation, expressed sometimes in the bitterest sarcasm, are both his strengths and his weaknesses. True, he is free from delusions about abstract truth and lives in a state of poetic emotionality and physicality; but all this seems to make him overly dependent on Didi for security, leadership, and rational direction. To use terms that the philosopher - psychoanalyst Erich Fromm has made vividly meaningful for us, Gogo is free from but not free to....

Since Beckett is deliberate and Occam - like in every area, we should note too the significance of the names he assigns. Estragon is French for tarragon, a wormwood grown for its pungent foliage which is used in making pickles and vinegar. The acerb yet earthy flavor fits Gogo's character perfectly. But Beckett is multi - lingual and international. While Estragon has its special appeal for French audiences, Go - Go has its value for English - speaking peoples. Gogo is the more restless one who always wants to go, go. But where? How? Why? When?

VLADIMIR

Of the two tramps, Didi is the one more committed to the rational side of man's nature. This is symbolized by his constant fussing with his hat. He is the more verbal of the two in the sense that he seems more concerned with precision in language, more willing to believe that language corresponds to reality. Didi seems more eager to present a good image to the outside world . . . he has greater social pride than Gogo and seems more susceptible to social embarrassment. Indeed, he is actually capable of anger over social injustice and the exploitation of the helpless by the powerful. All this helps explain why Didi seems to feel it is his duty to act as leader: an administrator relates to the outer world through objective, social logic, through verbal communication. Since Didi seems to believe in a higher world of the mind, he is predisposed to accept the existence of a higher reality outside himself, as represented, possibly, by Godot.

Still, we sense that the rational Didi is having a hard time keeping the lid on the irrational. That is the only way we can explain his impatience with his body - functions: he seems threatened by the fact that they are beyond the control of his mind. And we cannot avoid the implications of Didi's panic when Gogo tries to recount his dreams: Didi is denying the role of the unconscious in human life. Didi apparently is not coming to terms with his own subjective needs.

In this respect, consider his predicament over his belief in Godot. Didi acts as though loyalty to Godot will bring guidance, security, redemption, salvation. In other words, Didi believes these things can be "granted" from outside one's self. Didi is not alone in this hope. Man has always been counseled by his leaders to feel and act as though his center of gravity is outside himself. This is one of the central issues of the play. Suppose Godot does not come, or maybe doesn't even exist? That would mean, first of all, that Didi would have to find his meaning, his center of gravity, inside himself. And we are convinced, as we watch him, that he cannot come to terms with the inner Didi. Secondly, to admit that Godot is non-existent or even just indifferent would mean admitting that Didi has been basing the conduct of his friend and himself on an illusion. This is another awful possibility for a proponent of reason to have to face! Yet this seems to be the crux of the matter.

Consciously, of course, Didi thinks his belief in Godot is a rational belief. But his behavior obviously betrays a deep-down fear that maybe he has only rationalized a cherished dream. The greatest secret terror of all rationalists must be that they have willy-nilly used logic to "prove" what they want to believe.

Didi then is hobbled with self-contradictions. He seems to feel burdened by the responsibilities of "administering" this two-some in its passive vigil for Godot. Yet in waiting for Godot to solve his problems, Didi is irresponsibly "passing the buck." And in doing homage to objective reason, Didi denies the subjective nature and source of his need for Godot. And he uses belief in Godot to starve his own inner being. He might even, unconsciously, be using his belief in Godot to keep Gogo in bondage. Why else does Gogo put up with all this nonsense? The need to wait for Godot is the main restraint on Gogo.

With these reflections clearly in mind, we are prepared to contemplate the meaning of Didi's famous and beautiful soliloquy (pp. 58-58A), regarded by all critics as a gem of self-analysis. We sense that for a moment Didi has been caught off-guard by some unverbalized insight, a vision. Of what, really?

Does he for a moment see that he has been living a life of self-delusion? Does he for an instant see that the only way to break out of this Kierkegaardian anguish is to become Godot? But for Didi to see Didi as assuming Godot's responsibilities is to see Didi alone in a vast void of freedom, where each man makes himself, where each man becomes Man because he accepts the fact that he is on his own.

From the way the play ends, we infer Didi has lapsed back into self-delusion. He will go on waiting for Godot to come from the outside. He will panic tomorrow when Gogo tries to remember his dreams. Because Didi cannot admit to himself that he lives by a dream and calls it logic.

To return to Beckett's intentions in naming his characters - in Didi's case they are again international. Vladimir is a common Slavic name. Persons in the audience conversant with Russian history might see here an ironic **allusion**. Vladimir the Great (956-1015), ruler of Russia, was converted to Christianity and after his death was named St. Vladimir. The nickname Didi can sound to a French audience like dis - dis from the verb dire, to speak. Didi has put his faith in abstract concepts expressed through language. And "Speak - speak" has held "Go - Go" in restraint.

DIDI AND GOGO AS A COUPLE

From *Don Quixote* down to today's TV, we are familiar with that inseparable pair who seem to be together because they complement each other. In Willa Cather's *Death Comes for the Archbishop*, we have a productive relationship between an idealistic, visionary archbishop and a practical, canny priest. They collaborate like theory and practice to get things done with proper attention to both form and function. In the popular "Western," the twosome is likely to comprise a serious, high - minded leader and his comic side - kick; between them they represent both the puritanical and fun - loving attitudes toward life. The human question is, of course, simply this: Does the relationship make it easier for each of them to realize his own potential? If so, it is a creative, mutually liberating partnership. The archbishop is able to grow without violating his own nature; the priest has exactly the kind of work and freedom he is best suited for. In our typical cowboy pair, each seems to inspire the other to be himself. In such relations, opposites attract and challenge.

Literature teems, though, with examples of the other possibility: the pair who need each other, but stifle each other's growth, and yet cannot bear to part. As they weaken each other, the chances of independence grow slimmer. Their mutual dependence becomes a parasitic, symbiotic thing. Horace summed it up beautifully in his lines: "I can live neither with you nor without you." And Edward Albee achieved something of a miracle when, in *Who's Afraid of Virginia Woolf?*, he first created perfect types of this predicament in George and Martha and then managed to suggest, at the end, that whatever was creative in the attraction in the first place might still save it. Maybe.

Gogo and Didi are difficult to place on this spectrum. They certainly are opposites and certainly are mutually inter - dependent. Each day, as we have seen, they renew their relationship. For the rationally - oriented Didi would live a rarefied existence without his moody, earthy friend Gogo. The subjective Gogo would lack focus without his ostensibly objective side - kick Didi. Yet they are miserable much of the time together, returning always to the questions of suicide and separation, engaging always in neurotic tugs - of - war. Neither seems "big" enough to allow the other to be himself. In the bits of the action we have mentioned as essential to the interpretation, this is best represented in Didi's panicky interference with Gogo's dream - life, and in Gogo's draggy disparagement of Didi's rational pursuits.

Yet, whenever they become excited over the same thing, like an accurate description of a psychological state or a physical activity (see pp. 14A, 40A, 44A, et passim), they can collaborate like opera singers in a duet. In rapid alternation, they contribute words or phrases in a kind of stichomythy that is a Beckettian hallmark (see Beckett's Style). These passages are poignant examples of successful collaboration in the search for the quality of experience. They seem to be able to flourish as a couple but not as free individuals within a relationship. And no matter what happens, no matter what pleasure they briefly achieve, they return always to the sterile boredom of waiting for Godot.

Do they represent something special other than themselves? Their relationship surely is analogous to many pairings - off in society in which each party pays a heavy price for the dubious and intermittent benefits of the association. The classic example is the neurotic marriage, in which each party refuses to give up the other even while yearning for a rescuer. But the analogy can figure wherever specialization is forced on people. In division of labor, each individual is permitted to contribute only those aptitudes that are "needed" by the community; his other talents are left largely unexplored. While waiting for deliverance by Godot, the specialist can become a psychological paraplegic. Will Didi and Gogo go that far in their mutual stultification? Beckett seems to suggest they will unless they realize that Godot is in them.

GOGO AND DIDI AS PARTS OF A DIVIDED SELF

In studying the two tramps, we find it easier to regard them not as separate people but as parts of the same personality. There are indications in the play itself that this is Beckett's main intention. Why do the tramps spend the night apart? And why really can't they shake each other off? The answers become much easier when we see (1) Gogo as the Unconscious Mind, the ID, that part of the psyche related more to instinctive, irrational, primitive, non - verbalized forces in the human personality, and (2) Didi as the Conscious Mind, the Ego, that part of the psyche that is rational, verbal, social, and interested in "administering" the entire personality. This would explain why Didi and Gogo cannot separate once and for all. They are complementary parts of the same personality. Like "mind" and "body", no matter how incompatible they may be, they've got to stick it out, somehow. How do we know, then, what the total personality that consists of Didi + Gogo is like? The question sounds strange because when we think about it, we realize that in our memory of them, they do blend as one being. We accept their conflicts as we accept conflicts in our own Self.

Viewing Gogo and Didi as one personality does explain, moreover, why they can separate at night! When the total personality goes to sleep, so psychoanalysts tell us, the Ego relaxes and is off - guard. Then the Id, never inactive, has freer rein. As a consequence, the total personality experiences "dreams" in a language of private and racial symbolism. This is the "forgotten language," as Erich Fromm calls it, that rational man has long repressed. At night, then, Didi must relax and Gogo must be free of Didi's domination. When the total personality wakes, the Ego reasserts its control over the Id and, when necessary, represses it.

All of Didi's and Gogo's experiences . . . when they conflict and when they collaborate . . . make more sense in terms of the yoking of the Id and the Ego. Notice that we said that Didi and Gogo are happier when they combine their talents in a search for the quality of real experience. Beckett could be pointing out that given man's nature . . . with a mind divided between Conscious and Unconscious . . . his one hope is to bring them to focus like two eyes on the same experience. If the Conscious mind yearns after immutable essences outside itself, then the Unconscious withers. If the Unconscious takes over entirely, then man has ceased to be a rational animal. He becomes insane, like the man in the asylum that the hero of Murphy is playing chess with. But if Conscious mind enters into a fruitful collaboration with the Unconscious, tapping the latter's powerful energies and directing them to mutually beneficial aims, then both parts of the human personality can flourish. Beckett sees this collaboration, apparently, as possible only in the existentialist world, in which mind functions in and focuses on the unique present experience.

POZZO

From the moment he first arrives on stage, Pozzo impresses us as the personification of Raw Power. As we have noted in our summary of facts essential to interpretation, he owns all the surrounding terrain, he has a slave on a leash; we come to regard his whip as his attribute of power, his pipe as the symbol of his leisure. Most important, he acts like the nouveau riche at its most arrogant. His every action, every speech, seems to be based on cunning knowledge of how the world really works. Many of his remarks add up to disparagement of theory, a paraphrase of the adage that "It's not what you know, it's who you know." And that it's important to know Pozzo seems clear from his pompous emphasis on introduction. We must see here an oblique reference to the positivist's arrogant confidence in names and to the snobbish practice of name - dropping. Pozzo's acceptance of hypocrisy as a way of life that "pays off" is indicated by the way he winds up for "formal" pronouncements: manner, the official smile, seem far more important in his world than matter and genuine feeling.

Since our unmistakable impression of Pozzo's slave is that he is a well - educated man, we wonder, what does Beckett intend to signify by presenting a cultured person as a menial on a leash? Two historical analogies come to mind. The powerful, practical Romans conquered the cultured, theoretical, other - worldly Greeks. Great Greek thinkers wound up as slave - tutors in the households of nouveau riche Romans. An example closer to home (for Beckett and for students of literature) would be in the struggle that the Irish novelist George Moore had with the English booksellers. "At the head of English literature," wrote the embattled Moore, "sits a businessman." Do Pozzo and Lucky symbolize the businessman and the artist? Pozzo's arrogant attitude certainly smacks of the cynical idea that you don't need an education and a brain, all you need is the cunning to get people with brains on a leash.

Notice too Pozzo's concept of Time. Modern "practical" culture is based on "mechanical," astronomical time. But writers like Ambrose Bierce, Virginia Woolf, James Joyce, Henri Bergson have emphasized instead the reality of psychological time. By harnessing Nature and Humanity to work for Pozzo, Pozzo seems to have astronomical time well in hand.

Which brings us to the great mysterious change in Pozzo. He is still powerful when we meet him the second time. But he is now blind and disparages clock - time. Putting this new attitude into literary terms, we have to see that Pozzo has been "converted" by circumstances from objective, mechanical time, to subjective, psychological time. Ironically, now Pozzo cannot see his possessions. A Berkeleyan point here: if esse est percipi (to be is to be perceived), then Pozzo's possessions have lost much of their reality even to him.

What brought about the change in Pozzo? It's every critic's own guess. There is nothing in the play to indicate "motivation" or any relation between "cause and effect." Some critics infer that just "passing through" the world of Didi and Gogo infected Pozzo and Lucky with the tramps' despair. It seems to the present critic that Beckett is representing Pozzo's decline as the simple consequence of his way life. He has never had any roots that were his own. His entire vitality comes from exploiting people and things. Since the exploited get weaker, the exploiter weakens too. The Romans sucked Greek culture dry, into a "shell of truth." Then the Romans died out.

Again, in his naming, Beckett continues to emphasize the international. In naming Didi - and -Gogo, he has said something in French, English, Russian Now he adds Italian: in that language pozzo means a well. The very sound connotes a gusher, liquid coming up under pressure. And indeed Pozzo did have it "made," did "strike it rich," when he tapped the human resources of his slaves. But of course, even oil - wells run dry.

LUCKY

We must see the slave as a symbol of the Cartesian concept of man - as - a machine. Clearly a cultured being, as we have noted, Lucky has been reduced to the status of an automaton. Why has he accepted it? So far as we can infer, strictly for financial security. And noting the "progress" of the Pozzo -Lucky relation, we here see Beckett as representing the idea that slavery debases both slavery and slave -holder; that in "programming" another human being, the programmer is de - humanizing himself.

The contempt for thought that prevails in Pozzo's world is manifest in his commanding Lucky to "think" just as readily as he commands him to "dance." To the vulgar, the spectacle of a mind struggling for ideas is something to gape at, like the porpoise in the zoo jumping for the fish. And indeed Lucky's outburst, tirade, sermon . . . critics call it by different names, all inadequate . . . truly is a confounding performance. Critics vary too on the meaning they infer from this spate of language. Few doubt that this seeming gibberish is, on the surface at least, a **satire** on legalistic, scholarly, and scientific language, with all its hopeless and squeamish qualifications that pompously produce nothing definite. Few fail to catch Lucky's references to theological and philosophical questions as well. But let us emphasize here an interpretation not yet offered by other critics. If read carefully, Lucky's speech sounds less like the disconnected outpourings of a fine mind driven to lunacy, and more like the dithyrambic denunciations of the prophets. Better yet, it sounds more like the cryptic utterances of the Delphic Oracle, which the hearer had to interpret for himself.

This particular hearer . . . after repeated playings of the Columbia Masterworks recording of the work . . . detects in Lucky's outburst many dire threats to Pozzo's Establishment, threats calculated to get past him, perhaps, but not past others. Just as Rock poets use oblique language to get past the radio censors but still reach the Rock fan, so Lucky is using seeming gibberish to get past Pozzo but through to us. There are, for those set to hear it that way, omens of Conflagration and Deluge, and predictions of the rise of man against a materialistic regime and above a slide - rule approach to reality. But as we say, every critic has heard something different. One, alas, heard in Lucky's speech a **parody** of James Joyce's style. Critics inside the Establishment almost never do their homework.

In naming Lucky, Beckett has been, again, both international and ironic. There is a word for Lucky in every language, and it can be just as ironic in every tongue. Lucky is "lucky," as all slaves are considered lucky, to have somebody to take care of him. How else can a hungry intellectual eat, unless he becomes porter and valet to a man with power?

POZZO AND LUCKY AS A PAIR

Again, a pair of characters seem to suggest several kinds of pairing - off in our world. So far, we have seen Pozzo and Lucky simply as master and slave, or exploiter and exploited in an economic sense. But there is also a psychological symbolism here. Pozzo can symbolize the sadist, Lucky the masochist. That Lucky really enjoys being tortured is apparently made clear by the odd event we listed in our summary of essential action: when Gogo proffers a handkerchief to the weeping slave, Lucky kicks his would - be benefactor. This seems, of course, to indicate that Lucky wants no surcease from his masochistic ecstasy. But the situation resonates with other ironies. What else can Lucky do, except refuse a moment's solace from a stranger, in the presence of the master with whom he must go on "living"? Also, depending on how the director and the actor interpret this "bit," the audience might infer that Pozzo has "egged" Gogo on to get himself hurt. That Pozzo is a sadist, there is no doubt. That a slave must become a masochist, or else die in rebellion, is also worth considering. Our interpretation of Lucky's "oracle" surely suggests that he is playing two roles at once . . . while acting like the lucky lickspittle his master wants him to act like, he also does keep rebellion in mind. In this connection, consider what we may call a psychoeconomic interpretation of the kick: ... given no opportunity to express his resentment against his master directly, Lucky does take advantage of a chance to take out his frustrations in a way his master would approve of!

POZZO AND LUCKY AS PARTS OF A DIVIDED SELF

Pozzo and Lucky could also, like Didi and Gogo, be seen as parts of a divided self. Pozzo's contemptuous suppression of Lucky reminds us of the materialistic side of man rejecting and suppressing his spiritual and cultural heritage. This could explain, also, why Pozzo withers ... he has cut himself off from his roots.

THE MESSENGER

Minor as the messenger's role is in *Godot*, it does give us a perfect and compact example of Beckett's techniques of literary **allusion** and pervasive **irony**. In the first place, the audience knows from its experience with Greek drama that the arrival of a messenger signifies resolution. That missing piece of information, the final reaction, the awful **catastrophe** ... news of that kind is what the classical messenger brings. And so there is in *Godot* this ironic contrast, this deliberate let-down, because, as we have seen Godot's messenger brings no spectacular news, reveals nothing decisive in a "dramatic" sense. Secondly, he is not the worldly, experienced, or at least shrewd messenger of Greek drama, able to comment and elaborate on the news he brings, to answer questions about it, to fill in with background. No. Godot's messenger is a boy, a goat-boy. Thirdly, a casual autobiographical fact that the child yields up to Didi's questioning turns out to be the most important thing that Didi, in the long run, should know. Yet its significance is allowed to enter our awareness quietly, without dramatic fanfare.

Just as we need background in Greek drama to appreciate the new twist on the old messenger -technique, so we need background in the Hebraic - Christian culture to comprehend the full meaning of the casual fact that the goat - herd drops: his brother is a shepherd. Once we in the audience make the connection, we know that Didi is grappling with this too. For in the Gospel according to Matthew (chapter 25), Jesus the Shepherd says that when the "Son of Man comes in his glory, . . . he will separate men into two groups, as a shepherd separates the sheep from the goats, and he will place the sheep on his right hand and the goats on his left." For Didi, probably . . . for us, certainly . . . this brings back the whole cloudy question of arbitrary grace . . . God's preference for Abel over Cain, Isaac's preference for Esau over Jacob, Jesus' saving of only one of the two thieves crucified to the right and left of him . . . all of this long tradition summed up in that terrifying sentence from St. Augustine:

Do not despair, one thief was saved; do not presume, one thief was damned.

Why? Because one was born a goat, the other a sheep?

All of this resonates in our awareness as the boy stands there. This boy is the tramps' only contact with Godot. He is the intermediary between the human and the divine. He is, in short, priest - like. But notice, this priest is a goatherd! And in his attitudes, his innocence alone, this goat - boy unwittingly stresses that Godot's priest - messenger is a mere child from a world of fatherfigures, a world of arbitrary patriarchal justice. (Isaac did favor Esau, because he did eat of his meat.) Haven't we inferred from Didi's attitude, though, that in waiting for Godot, he is waiting for an ideal power? Now, deep down, poor conflictridden Didi has another suspicion to keep suppressed. Maybe Godot is not ideal but arbitrary.

And maybe by the time he comes for Didi and Gogo, which ones will then be in favor, the sheep or the goats, the "crux" on the right or the left?

GODOT AND HIS MESSENGER

Since Godot never appears on stage, we have the interesting artistic experience of constructing a character entirely in our own minds. Slowly the impression builds up that Godot is a being who makes appointments he does not keep and unconscionably postpones. He seems to be a pastoral figure, even a nomadic one; and the way the goat - boy acts, Godot could simply be his father: his pastoral, nomadic, patriarchal chieftain who (to a boy) would be a figure of unbelievable power. Is this the world Didi yearns for?

The brilliant Jungian analyst, Dr. Eva Metman, sees an awful significance in Godot's timing. Note, in our listing of the order of essential events, that the messenger arrives just in time to terminate any chance that Didi might reach full self - perception. Does Godot have a vested interest in keeping his followers off - balance, with their center of gravity outside themselves? Does Godot dislike the possibility that his children might free themselves from the Father?

GODOT AS THE UNMOVED MOVER

Godot has a strong resemblance to Aristotle's Unmoved Mover, who moves the Universe the way a beloved moves the lover. The Unmoved Mover is static, passive essence. In this connection, notice that Godot seems to exist only in the minds of static, passive creatures like Gogo, Didi, and the goat - boy. Is Godot simply an idealization of Didi's own way of life?

In any event, note again Beckett's neat trick of making the audience construct Godot entirely in the mind, demonstrating that Godot could well be nothing but a mental concept.

DOES GODOT APPEAR IN DISGUISE?

Acting on the hypothesis that man might not recognize the Ultimate Reality even if he met It face to face, we have to consider the possibility that Godot has appeared in disguise. Throughout history, gods have visited men in disguise. Because of the elaborate Christian background of *Waiting for Godot,* because of the assumption by now that this play is related to people waiting for the Second Coming, we are reminded of the stranger who meets the two disciples on the Road to Emmaus. "Something kept them from seeing who it was" (Gospel according to Luke, chapter 24.) It was, of course, the resurrected Jesus come to bolster the flagging spirits of his followers. On the Road to Nowhere in *Godot*, we surely have two men with flagging spirits; they are not going anywhere on the road, but then Beckett could of course be making another of his ironic contrasts here. But which of the characters that they meet on the road is the "stranger"?

It is fascinating to realize that each of the three persons that the tramps meet on the road could be a god(ot) in disguise as a stranger. Depending, of course, as Gorgias would remind us, on what the name Godot means to you!

Pozzo could be Godot if you think of God as arbitrary, vengeful, punitive. And Pozzo, as we have noted, is usually "made up" as a brazen idol!

Lucky could be Godot if you think of God as all - suffering and delivering his sermons in mysterious parables!

The goat - boy could be Godot if you think in terms of God as a child - god, innocent, pure, a new beginning for humanity.

And as a god(ot), each of these would require that you figure out for yourself what divinity really means and wants.

WHAT DOES THE WORD "GODOT" MEAN?

In French, the original language in which *Waiting for Godot* was written, the word for God is Dieu. But even French critics like Alain Robbe - Grillet have noted that *Godot* contains the "root" God from Beckett's native language. And as our discussion so far indicates, Godot certainly could be a personal God who keeps promising a Second Coming and never delivers. Or he could be an impersonal God, the Unmoved Mover, the Ultimate Reality, the Ultimate Idea, Pure Essence. To Didi, certainly, on the conscious level, Godot is Ideal Reality. But has Didi personified that Ideal? Has he misheard prophecies of the kind we ourselves might have misheard in Lucky's speech?

Hugh Kenner says that Beckett has told him about a French bicyclist, a professional racer, named Godeau. (The pronunciation would be the same as for Godot, namely, Go - Dough.) Godeau cycles here and there, and people don't really know when they'll see him again. Maybe today, maybe tomorrow. And Alan Schneider notes that godillot is French slang for boot. Is Gogo . . . with his concern for boots, which we have seen as concern for his roots in the earth . . . is Gogo the stranger in whom Didi cannot see the Godot he waits for? Is Gogo really Godot?

This kind of word - play is not the critic's doing, we must add. Contemporary art is much concerned with the esthetics of chance. That is, if the artist is likely to find no design in the universe, no meaning, he is likely to say that any chance order or coincidental arrangement at all has as much a chance as any of being the real one. Thus Joyce, Beckett's mentor, puts great faith in puns, especially since Freud tells us that puns play a major role in our dreams. Joyce, for example, had a picture of the Irish city of Cork hanging on his wall. The mount and the frame were made of cork. Everybody had to agree with Joyce that this was a picture of cork. And Beckett was overjoyed when he heard that his agent had his novel *Watt* under consideration at a new publisher's, named Watt & Watt. In artists who subscribe to the esthetics of chance, punning is a ritual. (See: Beckett's Style.)

In any event, we should go back to another Beckettian technique: the reductive one. Godot is that ideal power outside Didi which Didi believes will solve Didi's problems.

SUMMARY: HOW CHARACTERIZATION SIGNIFIES IN GODOT

Through spectacle, Beckett has cautioned us to start from nothing but time, space, and man in limbo. Through structure,

Beckett has impressed us that life is cyclical, spiraling downward, without progress or meaningful direction. How can we sum up what he has demonstrated through characterization?

In *Waiting for Godot*, Beckett has analyzed several different approaches to human fulfillment. He finds that all these approaches so far tried in the Western world have failed to bring man any measure of happiness. The one approach still not tried is the one Beckett believes that man needs and is yearning for. It is the only one that might still bring him his full realization as Man.

Pozzo and Lucky dramatize the futility of seeking fulfillment in the physical world. Pozzo, through his will, drives himself and others in the fierce activity of gaining power over people and possessions. Lucky, because he lacks will and economic security as well, participates in this frantic race. Lucky is intellectual by nature, but his real talents are wasted because a world run by Pozzo is a world in which only things count. In violating his own nature for the mere "leavings" of the master's table, in adjusting to Pozzo's system, Lucky himself becomes a thing.

Looking outside the play to see what the Lucky - Pozzo world might represent, we see analogies not only in such power - systems of the past as the Egyptian and Roman Empires, but also in both of the two major power - systems today. Both communism and capitalism are basically materialistic in their values. Khrushchev, ex - premier of Soviet Russia, once declared that communism's goal was to produce more pigs than capitalism could produce.

Didi and Gogo, taken as a pair, dramatize the futility of passively waiting for fulfillment in some ideal world. They seem to represent, as individuals, the rational and irrational forces in man. If Pozzo and Lucky are seen as locked in internecine economic conflict, then Didi and Gogo can represent mankind engaged in paralyzing psychological conflict. Exhausted and stultified by their neurotic interplay, they are waiting for a rescuer to come like a bolt from the blue.

They too represent strong historical forces. Throughout history, throughout art, mankind has waited for a saviour. The earliest full - length work that can be called part of English literature is an **epic** poem about King Hrothgar who languishes while waiting for the impossible . . . a disinterested saviour from out there. Of course, the impossible happens. Beowulf arrives! In later medieval times, all Europe contemplated the arrival of a knight so pure he could reach the Chapel Perilous and retrieve the Holy Grail. Every night, TV reaffirms our cherished belief that some Deerslayer, Lone Ranger, or Paladin will gallop in out of nowhere and clean up the town. So Didi waits in good company. As Henry David Thoreau said, "Most men lead lives of quiet desperation." (Italics ours.) And one of the most beautiful melodies in world music was composed by Handel to impress in our minds forever a (mistranslated) line from the Book of Job:

I know that my Redeemer liveth.

And John Milton ended a famous **sonnet** with the line:

They also serve who only stand and wait.

Ironically, Milton did not only stand and wait. Even in his blindness, he worked hard for both artistic and political causes. The **irony** is greater when we realize that John Milton also believed in a Saviour, but he felt he should help out in the case of his own personal salvation.

Both these approaches . . . the Pozzo - Lucky search in the physical world and the Didi - Gogo search in an ideal world . . . have one thing in common. In both cases, the goal, the yearned - for reality, is located outside the Self. Gogo, a kind of personification of the Id, senses that there is a universe inside himself worth exploring; but Didi, a rough personification of the Ego, is terrified by the Unconscious and succeeds in directing their mutual aspirations toward Godot. Similarly, Lucky, a **parody** of culture in a state of decay, is prevented by his materialistic master from following his own intellectual bent. A psychoanalyst would say that not only Didi and Gogo, but also Pozzo and Lucky, all have in common the fact that they are fleeing from themselves. A science - fiction aficionado might quip that man's recoil from Inner Space is enough to power him through Outer Space.

Idealism, that is, philosophical dualism with belief in a second world of values higher than the world of matter; materialism, or the philosophical belief that there is nothing but the physical world . . . both these approaches fail in Beckett's play. The possibility of a third approach shapes up briefly (and this is significant) in the mind of Didi. He comes close to seeing that the ideal world, symbolized by Godot, can be found in himself. From Ralph Waldo Emerson's *Oversoul* to many Oriental philosophies to modern Existentialism, this makes sense. They may disagree on whether there is a God outside man, but they all agree that God is in man.

But Didi shrinks back, and the reason is clear. He has excluded his Unconscious from his personality. Didi and Gogo could experience Godot only through harmonious interaction of the rational and irrational power in themselves.

If this analysis has any validity, we may infer that *Waiting for Godot* says in effect that man will remain in a state of paralysis until he can:

unite his divided psychological self;

end his internecine struggle for economic power over people and property;

cease searching for fulfillment in either an ideal world or in the physical world, both being outside himself;

and begin instead searching for fulfillment in himself.

BECKETT'S STYLE AND THE NEW CATHARSIS

An artist's style is his own unique, characteristic way of expressing himself through his art media. As unanalyzable as his personality, the artist's style is a blend of many factors... his attitudes and emphases; his way of "leaning" into his material; his choice of old techniques and creation of new ones; the nature of the **themes** he tackles; his use of influences and response to the Zeitgeist (spirit of the times), and so on. In the case of a dramatist, his style is the resultant of his peculiar blending of spectacle, symbols, structure, characterization, language and **genre** to say what he has to say, at his pace, in his way.

In spectacle, as we have seen, Beckett is boldly reductive and symbolic; through spectacle, he has represented Man as facing the Void; he satirizes action as an illusion and stresses the stasis and stagnation of human existence. Through his highly original structure, he dramatizes the circularity of life;

by denying crisis and the conventional "insight of catharsis," he has emphasized the quality of human experience that remains when these contrived events have been eliminated: the quality of tedium, emptiness, alienation. In his creation of characters, Beckett again is reductive and symbolic, yet warmly human, showing that whether a man chooses the active or the passive way (selling a serf or waiting for Godot), he cannot long escape the knowledge that nothing ever is really perceived, achieved, or communicated. How much, then, of Beckett's total effect can we attribute to the remaining two components of style . . . his choice and use of a **genre**, and his use of language: that is, his literary style?

WAITING FOR GODOT AS TRAGICOMEDY

In classical drama, tragedy and comedy were distinctly different. While there was some mild "comic relief" in some tragedies, every Greek tragedy was predominantly tragic in tone; its catharsis was achieved solely through acceptance of the outcome as lamentable but inevitable. Comedy, while it had its serious overtones, was still overwhelmingly gay and provocative of uproarious laughter. In Renaissance drama, though, a greater blend of these two modes developed, called tragicomedy: a strong mixture of the lamentable and the laughable. In drama of the late Shakespearean period, the ending of a tragicomedy was in doubt for so long into the play, the "happy ending" was achieved by such sudden reversals, that the audience was left with a knowledge of the fragility of happiness. Shakespeare's own "bitter comedies" kept the audience reminded of the intimate relation between extreme opposites! And contemporary tragicomedy is very likely not to have even the happy ending that tragicomedy is supposed to offer.

Why these shifts in emphasis from "pure" tragedy and "pure" comedy to various blends of tragicomedy? The modern temperament, as we have noted, would distrust terms like "tragic" and "comic" as absolutes. Obviously, what is a happy ending for the **protagonist** is an unhappy ending for the antagonist, and if I've been more sympathetic to one than to the other, that's because the author has shaped my interests that way. And like Graham Greene, modern man is likely to feel that if any of us is going to be damned, we should all be (interested in the) damned. Or to put it in terms of Conrad's "shadow line," all heroes are secret sharers in the guilt of the villains. Sympathy in modern art shifts from the hero to the victim and the anti - hero if not all the way to the so - called outlaw. The modern artist distrusts "success" as usually defined, and is more concerned with "failure" as we have discussed that word earlier.

Another consideration: tragedy is usually seen as a consequence of a hero's being subjected to irreconcilable claims or pressures. If Antigone disobeys the king's decree and buries her brother, she is damned as a traitorous citizen; if she obeys the king and leaves her brother unburied, she is damned by the gods for familial disloyalty. Antigone is a real tragic figure in the classic sense; her conflict and fate are supposed comprehensible because of the context and nature of the situation. But again, the modern temperament looks askance first of all at the very validity of these claims on her; secondly, at the contrived balance between the two claims.

For the modern writer, almost every subject or situation is inherently ironic and dramatic precisely because it can be both tragic and comic, depending on point of view... which itself will change and which always, in any event, will be distorted and partial. The only truthful drama is tragicomedy or comitragedy. "Light," says the dramatist Eugene Ionesco, "makes shadow deeper, and shade accentuates the light. I personally have never understood the distinctions between the comic and the tragic. Since the comic is the intuition of the absurd, then the comic seems to me to be more hopeless than the tragic." Except, we might add, that comedy makes it possible to shrug our shoulders and go on living.

We can see why Beckett would find tragicomedy the most natural **genre** for his dramatic representation of the confusion, ambiguity, and absurdity of modern life. We can see why he, like so many contemporaries, rediscovers the high artistic value of so-called "low" comedy. We laugh at the antics of the two tramps so that we may not cry. We may not solve our dilemmas but at least we are not going to trade them in for delusions. Traditional catharsis may not be granted us, in our time; but perhaps we do experience a new kind of catharsis. More of that later.

BECKETT'S LITERARY STYLE

All writers have to learn to control their literary talents if they are to succeed in writing for the stage. In Shakespeare's early plays, he luxuriates in language. Indeed, passionate belief in the validity of language was quite in the spirit of the Renaissance. Even so, in his later plays, Shakespeare "tamed" his poetic instincts to make his language more functional, more dramatic. Beckett went through this development in a different way. He did his "luxuriating" in his early fiction, and he came to drama (as he came to his later fiction) with language thoroughly under control. He is as Occam-like, as reductive, in his purely literary techniques as he is in his use of spectacle and structure. This is indicated in the various drafts that his works go through. The first draft of Fin de Partie was longer, more detailed than the last; when Beckett recreated the work in English as *Endgame*, he reduced its proportions even further. In this respect he is, like Hemingway and many other moderns, a follower of Mallarme, who said that "To state is to destroy, to suggest is to create." Beckett's language is so reduced to the core that it becomes utterly impossible to describe it or even quote it out of context without losing most of its quality. It is, truly, existentialist language in the sense that it means only in context. With these caveats and disclaimers in mind, it must be clear that the specific observations that follow are intended to stimulate the student to a new hearing of the recording or a new reading of the play (for this purpose, we again provide page numbers of passages that illustrate our points).

The main criterion for dramatic dialogue is, of course, that the language suit the character of the person speaking it. And when an author throws different personalities together, he is called upon to write many different kinds of language to express their different and changing attitudes. It is in meeting such needs that Beckett proves himself a master of language resources.

Notice that when we remember Didi's speech, we remember that it is he who tries to state a problem fully in language, and to pursue it with language (for example, pp. 9-9A, 51-52); it is Didi who searches for the right word (pp. 8, 9); who attempts the sententious epigram (p. 8) and re - states Hamlet's dilemma (To be or not to be, that is the question) in parallel language that explicitly declares the difference in the **themes** of the two plays (p. 51a). And it is Didi who almost "breaks through" by first posing questions in logical, albeit useful, fashion (pp. 58-58A). Didi's language, from the most casual to the most passionate, is the language of the struggle for clarity. But when we remember Gogo's speech, we recall that it is he who is more likely to proceed not by logic but by free association (p. 11A); it is Gogo who abandons "adult" language and uses a combination of baby

- talk and (apparently) pantomime when an idea becomes too difficult to verbalize (p. 12A); Gogo who unquestioningly uses only pantomime when that seems more effective (p. 11A); Gogo who invokes an euphemism (p. 8A), a proverb (p. 12A), and even a Heraclitean precept (p. 39) mainly as the basis for a pun or a **parody**. We recall that it is in Gogo's voice that we hear both the "grosser," more violent feelings (pp. 32A, 39A) and the more poignantly naive ones expressed (p. 44A). Gogo's language, from the most casual to the most passionate, is the language of acceptance of chaos, acceptance of obscurity.

Yet, when these two cease sniping at each other and begin collaborating, their languages blend into one. Didi gives up his more complex **syntax**, Gogo gives up his simple declarative sentences, and they match each other's word for word, phrase for phrase, or sentence for sentence (pp. 13, 14A, 17A, 25A, 40A, 49) in spontaneous parallelism, in a mutual effort to agree on the quality of experience. In these beautiful "duets," Beckett uses a kind of stichomythy all his own. It was the Greek dramatic poets who developed this technique. As the action stepped up in tempo, the characters spoke shorter speeches; at the height of tension, they would exchange a line for a line (stichomythia) in rapid give - and - take. As the tension relaxed, their speeches would lengthen again. Note that in *Waiting for Godot*, Beckett reverses this. He uses stichomythy not for the peak of conflict but for the height of harmony. (However, in *Endgame* he uses stichomythy the way the Greeks did.) These stichomythic passages are the best in which to study Beckett's control over the music of language. Notice how in these passages cited he employs **alliteration** or initial **rhymes** (balancing words that start with the same sound, as in slob and slave); dissonance or the rhyming of consonants only (as in giggling and haggling); and feminine endings (concluding lines on unaccented syllables, giving the effect of a sad "let - down:" as on robber, horror, lover).

Many of these stichomythic passages can be "scanned" as verse, and indeed have to be rendered as such by the actors.

Once having appreciated the musical quality of the stichomythic passages, we are prepared to notice that every speech that Beckett writes is precisely cadenced and vocalized (that is, the vowels are carefully chosen and arranged for their sound effects). Actors and directors were originally amazed at the frequency with which Beckett's stage directions call for a pause or a change of pace. They discovered that even his silences are part of his communication. His Come and Go is a play of only 121 spoken words! As Martin Gottfried has noted, "the play's strength is in the unspoken." This helps to explain Beckett's popularity among the younger generation who distrust conventional belief in . . . and hypocritical use of . . . words, words, words.

Which reminds us that in *Waiting for Godot*, it is Pozzo who can affect a lyrical outburst or "put on" a formal, public presentation (pp. 20A, 22A, 25-25A); it is Pozzo too who delivers one of the most anguished cries in our dramatic literature (p. 57A). In his first appearance, then, Pozzo is the man who glibly "uses" language for facile effect, as do demagogues, advertisers, propagandists, and circus barkers. But in his second appearance, language comes painfully to him, and then it erupts out of him, like bile.

And of course, when we remember Lucky, we recall that fantastic tirade, that sermon - like **parody** on sermons, that oracular diatribe, that spate of apparent gibberish that expresses, in distorted and fractured language, all that Lucky has had to suppress.

What we remember, then, is that each character has a speech of his own that still varies as he varies. In creating that language for each character, Beckett has shown mastery over a great range of literary devices, all the way from lowly pun and simple parallelism to haunting dissonance and sustained lyricism.

BECKETT AND THE "NEW CATHARSIS"

What does the avant-garde dramatist like Beckett offer his audience in place of the "catharsis" provided by the traditional dramatist? How does the total effect of *Waiting for Godot* compare with the total effect of a conventional play?

Traditionally, catharsis is seen as both an intellectual and an emotional process. Intellectually, the audience is made aware of a problem and then sees the problem resolved. The ending may be "unhappy" or tragic, but the dramatist has demonstrated that given the circumstances and the makeup of the people involved, the outcome was inevitable. Thus the audience is reassured that reason and order are the ultimate reality. Emotionally, as Aristotle first observed, the audience has been aroused to sensations like pity and terror; then the ending of the play has purged the audience of those emotions before they leave the theater. In other words, the classical ideal is that the audience goes home (or turns off the TV) chastened, re-adjusted to the status quo, accepting Fate and the wisdom of things as presently understood. The ideal aim here has been to restore Apollonian balance and harmony.

Not every contemporary dramatist can accept these definitions of his function. Why should he design, in each play, a new type of "safety valve" to relieve psychological and social pressures that maybe should not be so deflected and deflated?

Why shouldn't he, when he deems it more honest and therefore more artistic, rather build up those pressures, intensify them until they become so unbearable that the audience must recognize them for what they really are? Notice too that the only kinds of problems likely to be taken up in the theater of traditional catharsis are by definition the kinds of problem that can be "resolved." Obviously these are not the great fundamental problems that are most urgent precisely because they remain unresolved or even unrecognized.

Beckett certainly is not interested in sending us away chastened, satisfied, back where we started, just one play older. He wants us rather to go away "with a slow burn," aware that some cherished illusions have been weighed and found weightless. Beckett does not want us to be intellectually reassured by the rationality of it all; he wants us to be appalled and shaken by the absurdity of it all. Certainly he doesn't want us to resolve problems on the intellectual and emotional levels, he wants us to respond as unified selves: he feels that our self - dichotomizing is one of our greatest unrecognized problems.

It is highly likely that the many people who walked out at the end of the first act of the Miami production of *Godot* were the people most affected, most panicked or numbed, the ones least able to absorb such an assault on their delusions. They are the ones who go to the theater to be reassured that life, as they lead it and glorify it, adds up to something. Seeing two tramps dawdling away the time was too much like catching a glimpse of themselves going through their own absurd routines. Truth is what they go to the theater to forget.

But those in the audience who can survive the initial impact of a Beckett play are fortunate enough to experience a new kind of catharsis. We enjoy a tremendous relief at being disabused of complex irrelevancies and outmoded "solutions." We experience that exhilarating release that comes of knowing that at last we are keeping the real problems in focus. Instead of Apollonian balance, harmony, reassurance from the outside, we experience now a new state of Heraclitean awareness, disenchanted maybe with old views of the nature of things, but aware of restless new responsibilities inside.

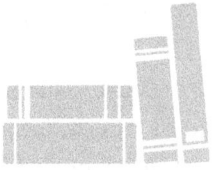

WAITING FOR GODOT

SURVEY OF CRITICISM

An extraordinary literature has sprung up about *Waiting for Godot* and its author. Few works of art have touched off such voluminous and spirited response so soon after their initial presentation. A clue to the integrity of Beckett's art is the quality of this criticism: he has challenged some of the major critics and has elicited their best work. A comprehensive bibliography of Beckett criticism has not yet been attempted; it would surely run to several thousand items. For our purposes here, it will be valuable to survey and sample this literature under four headings: (1) early reviews of performances; (2) full - length critical studies; (3) case - books and anthologies of critical essays; and (4) treatises on contemporary drama. Full bibliographical data will be found in Further Reading.

EARLY REVIEWS OF PERFORMANCES

Paris

En Attendant Godot was first performed in the small auditorium of the Theatre de Babylone in Paris in January, 1953. Typical of the enthusiastic response . . . and most prophetic of all . . . was the opinion of Sylvain Zegel, who wrote:

Theatre - lovers rarely have the pleasure of discovering a new author worthy of the name; an author who can give his dialogue true poetic force, who can animate his characters so vividly that the audience identifies with them; who, having meditated, does not amuse himself with mere word juggling; who deserves comparison with the greatest. . . . In my opinion Samuel Beckett's first play *Waiting for Godot,* at the Theatre de Babylone, will be spoken of for a long time.

Indeed, *Godot* was the talk of intellectual Paris all that year, running for more than 300 performances. One constant **theme** of that early discussion, in both the cafe and the intellectual journal, was the religious significance of *Godot*. For example, for Edith Kern, *Waiting for Godot* glorified "the all -surpassing power of human tenderness" which she saw as the substitute for the Redeemer who never comes and for whom man waits in vain.

London

English - speaking audiences, which had not seen as much avant - garde drama as had the Parisians, reacted with mixed feelings. Harold Hobson concluded his review in the *London Times* by saying: "Go and see *Waiting for Godot.* At the worst you will discover a curiosity, a four - leaved clover, a black tulip; at the best something that will surely lodge in a corner of your mind for as long as you live." And an anonymous critic, writing for the *Times Literary Supplement,* saw *Godot* as a "modern morality play on permanent Christian themes," a play that represents the "tension and uncertainty in which the average Christian must live in this world." But the American critic, Marya Mannes, wrote acidly about the same London production:

> The play concerns two tramps who inform each other and the audience at the outset that they smell. It takes place in what appears to be the town dump, with a blasted tree rising out of a welter of rusting junk, including plumbing parts. They talk gibberish to each other and to two 'symbolic' maniacs for several hours, their dialogue punctuated every few minutes by such remarks as 'What are we waiting for?,' 'Nothing is happening,' and 'Let's hang ourselves.' The last was a good suggestion, unhappily discarded.

And surveying the London theatre for an American quarterly, Bonamy Dobree said flatly about *Godot* in particular:

> ... it is time to affirm that anything that can be called art must ultimately be in praise of life, or must at least promote acceptance of life, thus indicating some values.

Dobree thus epitomized the widely - accepted view of the time that Beckett's work, because of its "nihilism," cannot "be called art."

Miami and New York

The American productions of 1956 ... the "flop" in Miami and the carefully publicized "success" in New York ... drew sympathetic comment from many leading critics. Kenneth Rexroth ... a perceptive critic who must be credited with calling Louis Zukofsky "great" a decade before everybody was doing it ... saw *Godot* as a plea for universal brotherhood. The comradeship of men, he said, whether verminous tramps with unmanageable pants or Jim and Huck Finn drifting through all the universe on their raft ... the comradeship of men in work, in art, or simply in waiting, in the utterly unacquisitive act of waiting. . . is an ultimate value, so ultimate that it gives life sufficient dignity and satisfaction.

And Horace Gregory, another poet and historian of poetry, saw Beckett's characters as resembling Roman gladiators because they live outside the **conventions** of society. Didi and Gogo's sacrifice, Gregory said, is not tragic, it is simply anonymous, made in vain. Seeking the origins of Beckett's attitudes in Beckett's own life - circumstances, Gregory decided that Beckett's having been brought up as a Protestant in Southern Ireland had made him feel alienated from society.

The New York cast, as we have noted earlier, recorded its interpretation and William Saroyan, playwright and novelist, wrote the "Introduction" for the Columbia Masterworks album. Saroyan found that Beckett had studied one "bleak and comic inch of truth" so intensively that "it finally gives the appearance of being nearly the whole world," and the play becomes "very nearly the whole true fable of man." Taking up the question of the absence of women in *Godot*, Saroyan noted that Beckett "may have meant that one or all of the men are women, . . . or that waiting is exclusively male, or always male - and -female, or entirely neutral." And striking a kind of American - Existentialist pose, Saroyan declared that *Godot* "means what it means to whoever is watching, listening, or reading. What else could it possibly mean?"

FULL - LENGTH STUDIES OF BECKETT

Within a decade of the first English performance of *Godot*, several major full - length studies of Beckett's work were in print. One of the earliest and still one of the best is Hugh Kenner's *Samuel Beckett: A Critical Study* (1961), a breath - taking for both its literary insights, the philosophical relations it establishes, and the brilliance with which it is written. Kenner lays the ground - work for the student's understanding of Descartes' world as Beckett has explored it: a world in which man is both a machine and a user of machines. "The Cartesian Centaur is a man riding a bicycle." Kenner also establishes the importance in Beckett of man as both a chess - player and a chess - piece. Frederick J. Hoffman's *Samuel Beckett: The Language of Self* demonstrates that the philosophical ground of contemporary literature has "shifted from **metaphysical** to epistemology. Characters who were formerly maneuvered within an accepted frame of extra - literary reference are now ... seeking their own language."

Hoffman concluded that Beckett brings the "language of the self" to an "inescapable impasse." He takes the self as a starting point, subordinates all of the vast and systematic orders of **metaphysical** explanation to the position of a cluster of **metaphors** available to the inquiring self, and proceeds then to a narrative and dramatic series of meditations upon them.

Hoffman sees *Waiting for Godot* as Beckett's "best play (and one of the best of all contemporary plays)." *Godot*, according to Hoffman, contains Beckett's "essential 'doctrine,'" namely, that

> ... life consists of "waiting," ... It is an agony to "wait for Godot" in a place deprived of almost all recognizable natural promise and from a point - of - view all but deprived of confidence. But we ... must go on ... unquestioning ... unbelieving ...

Ruby Cohn's *Samuel Beckett: The Comic Gamut* and William York Tindall's *Samuel Beckett* are also indispensable for the student of Beckett, Cohn because of her poetic sensitivity to analogies and sources, Tindall because he is a great Joyce scholar who has followed Beckett's career from his earliest days as a Joyce disciple.

CASEBOOKS AND CRITICAL ANTHOLOGIES

Some of the most valuable exegeses of Beckett are contained in collections of critical essays. Martin Esslin has edited *Samuel Beckett* which contains the famous Kenner chapter on "The Cartesian Centaur," a Cohn essay on Beckett's sources in philosophy, and a profound Jungian study of *Godot* by Dr. Eva Metman. Esslin's own introduction provides a good Kierkegaardian background for Beckett. Ruby Cohn has edited her own Casebook on *Waiting for Godot*. Several essays in a third collection, *Endgame*, edited by Bell Gale Chevigny, are relevant for the student of *Godot* . . . especially Alan Schneider's "Waiting for Beckett: A Personal Chronicle."

TREATISES ON MODERN DRAMA

Although no treatise on modern drama published since 1960 ignores Beckett, there are five especially that command the student's attention, for widely different reasons. Frederick Lumley's Trends in Twentieth Century Drama sums up perfectly the horror of the conventional critic over *Waiting for Godot*:

> . . . it seems to this writer that this play is more akin to a cesspool of the degradations of human souls than a tragedy of misfortune. Is there no limit to the depths to which man may descend and is there so little faith left in man that he must lie here forgotten? Will he never be given a resurrection, will we never again have new horizons opened to us through the nobility of man, and be

able to enter a world not altogether unlike our own where there is no exploitation of facile optimism or morbid despair?

Lumley's book, then, has the dubious distinction of providing the student with valuable historical background on the position of the Establishment in matters theatrical. More realistic, more modern in attitude, is George Wellwarth's *The Theatre of Protest and Paradox: Developments in the Avant - Garde Drama*. In highly readable and often witty language, Wellwarth studies Beckett's plays against the background of his novels and in the trend represented by Alfred Jarry, Antonin Artaud, Arthur Adamov, and Eugene Ionesco. Wellwarth believes that the "deterministic philosophy that underlies all of Beckett's work is most clearly exemplified" in his plays. For the reader of this Monarch Guide, Wellwarth will be valuable because he takes a position diametrically opposed to ours. Beckett, he says,

has drawn one of the two possible conclusions from the perception that the universe is unknowable. The other conclusion ... that the world as it is, is worthwhile for the simple reason that it is all that there is (that Being in any form is better than Nonbeing, in other words) is Camus'. Beckett is the prophet of negation and sterility. He holds out no hope to humanity, only a picture of unrelieved blackness; and those who profess to see in Beckett signs of a Christian approach or signs of compassion are simply refusing to see what is there.

Strongly disagreeing with Professor Wellwarth is the young working critic, Martin Gottfried. In his first book, *A Theatre Divided,* Gottfried declared that "Beckett's plays are ... thoroughly optimistic." Gottfried was one of the first to hail *Waiting for Godot*, which he described in this book as "one of the most significant plays written during the twentieth century," offering "a new way of looking at things." In his second book, *Opening*

Nights, Gottfried discusses Beckett's influence on Harold Pinter. "Like Beckett, he emphasizes uncertainty by limiting himself to only the certain and showing how it is not enough and yet all we have to go on." Gottfried concludes his book in a way that suggests that he is trying to develop a Beckettian technique of dramatic criticism. Like Beckett, Gottfried sees a need for a new **syntax**, for new ways of making critical language get down to the fundamentals. Gottfried should be watched as one of the most original critics of our time.

The most ambitious - yet, in some ways, the most profound - treatise on modern drama recommended for students of Beckett is Tom F. Driver's *Romantic Quest and Modern Query*. Herein Beckett is viewed in a cavalcade of "greats" from Goethe and Kleist down to Brecht and Genet. "The roots of modern tragicomedy lie in Chekhov, the first important playwright to make art out of the representation of the qualities of life rather than its actions," Driver reminds us. "His innovations made possible a purely theatrical theater, of which the modern epitome has been reached in the plays of Samuel Beckett." Driver sees *Waiting for Godot* as "not only a masterpiece, but also the quintessence of modern tragicomedy," and a major factor in Beckett's winning the 1969 Nobel Prize for Literature. In Beckett's plays, notes Driver, the

> ... social setting has entirely disappeared, and what remains is only a model of the consciousness of Western man, exhausted by history and longing for death, yet not able to imagine ... the surcease of that which is his glory and his damnation ... namely, his pellucid self - awareness.

With Beckett, the development of modern theater, in reaching its epitome, seems also to have come to an end.... The theater now casts about for a new way to travel.

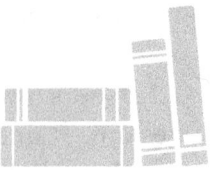

OTHER PLAYS

ENDGAME

INTRODUCTION

Most clearly related to *Godot* . . . in **theme**, technique, **genre** - is the play *Endgame*, which we shall therefore analyze at some length. And for certain specific ways in which they throw additional light on both *Godot* and *Endgame*, we should discuss briefly two other dramatic works . . . Krapp's *Last Tape* and *All that Fall* . . . as well as *Three Novels: Molloy, Malone Dies.*

HISTORY OF THE PLAY

After a long period of painful suffering from "writer's block" . . . during which he came to believe he had run dry as an artist . . . Beckett finally completed *Fin de Partie* in 1956. He followed with an English version of the play, *Endgame*, by which time he was well - launched on his second great burst of radical originality. But in spite of the historic success of *Godot,* no Paris theater - manager was willing to risk the premiere production of the much starker *Fin de Partie*. Accordingly, the play was tried out in England; the first French performance was given in the Royal

Court Theatre in London, on April 3, 1957. In May, the French text was published, and then the stage production, under new sponsorship, ran in Paris for almost 100 performances. On October 28, 1958, the English version opened in London with Krapp's *Last Tape* on the same bill. Meanwhile, Alan Schneider, the New York producer, had spent much time in Paris with Beckett preparing for the American production, which enjoyed a successful run at the Cherry Lane Theater.

Critical reaction to Beckett's second full - length play was sharply divided. The French critics were fervently enthusiastic or fervently angry. The London critics were either baffled or disappointed, with the exception of Harold Hobson, who called *Endgame* "a magnificent theatrical experience." In New York, the preview performances were joyously received; Brooks Atkinson wrote an excellent appreciation of the play; Walter Kerr was quite "respectful"; several critics returned for a second viewing. And in its handsome Grove Press paperback format, *Endgame* has come to be regarded ... like *Godot* ... as "must" reading by the new generation in the theater.

NATURE OF THE ACTION

The action of *Endgame* is grim, moving, and extraordinarily compact. Overtly, the action proceeds simply along one continuous line of development; yet subliminally at least, the play can be experienced on many levels of meaning. In order to interpret the spectacle, structure, and characterization, it is necessary to remind ourselves of these essential facts about the action:

In a bleak interior, Clov (physically unable to sit), takes care of blind Hamm (in an armchair on castors) and Hamm's legless parents, Nagg and Nell (in ash‑cans). Today, as every day, Hamm engages in acrimonious dialogue with Clov (his servant; his son?). Main topic: Will Clov leave Hamm? Hamm orally composes another scene of a first‑person narrative. Clov sights a boy outside. Hamm puts a handkerchief over his face, Clov stands dressed at the door, and... Curtain. Does Clov leave?

SIGNIFICANCE OF THE SPECTACLE AND SITUATION

The bleak interior suggests, at various times in the action, (1) a corner of a chess‑board, (2) the inside of a skull, (3) the interior of a bomb shelter, (4) the interior of Noah's Ark, and (5) a stage. (1) The physical arrangement and attitudes of the characters (as well as the title of the play) suggest chessmen trapped in one corner of the board and playing out their final, hopeless moves. In chess, the king is the piece whose capture ends the game; he must thus be protected in depth; by himself he is incapable of any extensive, major action, because he is allowed to move only one space in any direction. This gives him, at the most, only nine squares of potential movement from his present position. Hamm seems to be the king in this endgame. His armchair suggests a "throne," and its movement on castors suggests the terribly limited maneuvers a king can make. Clov, in constant motion and unable to "descend," reminds us of the knight forever "mounted" on a horse. Indeed, without one such mobile piece left, King Hamm could not last many moves more. Nagg and Nell, since they are totally immobilized, can be any two pieces pinned down by the opposing player. Seen as a chess‑game, this "play" doesn't have long to go... except for one remote possibility. (2) The action can also be viewed, and experienced, as a conflict inside the mind of one person. The four characters are then seen as conflicting parts of one personality.

Clov seems to represent the Ego, the psyche's caretaker and contact with the outside world; Hamm, the Id, the blind, self-centered, irrational force of the psyche; and Nagg and Nell, the Super-Ego, that internalized voice of the parents that may be experienced as a nagging conscience. Since the boy is outside this conflict-ridden mind, he may be experienced as a symbol simply of the world outside; or as a symbol of the apparently unified Self that another person always seems to be when viewed externally; or as a symbol of the new Self that the mind-in-conflict perceives and hopes to reach. Does Clov leave? becomes then a question about whether Clov actually does make contact with another person or with a new Self. (3) The bleak interior also resembles a disaster shelter; the excitement over the boy increases our feeling that very little life has survived outside these walls. (4) Since the Biblical Ham was a son of Noah, and since these people seem cooped up during a catastrophe and excited over the possibility of life outside, we witness the scene with strong reminders of Noah's Ark: are we in the cabin? Has Ham superseded Noah? Has the Ark foundered? (5) Since the name Hamm also suggests both "ham" actor and Hamlet, and since his speeches are self-dramatizing to say the least, the impression grows on us that so far as he is concerned, this is a play and the setting is a stage. This ties in with any or all of the other settings we can experience: for if Hamm is that part of the fragmented mind that represents fantasy and subjectivity, then he imagines scenes as well as composes stories. He can imagine himself as Ham the son of Noah, or as a King besieged. We are reminded, throughout the subjectivist literature of the last century, that the mind is a stage on which fantasies are enacted.

These various spectacles also interrelate in other ways. Consider the medieval view of man (or human nature) as the epitome of the world or the universe: that is, of man as the microcosm of the macrocosm. Viewed that way, the spectacle of *Endgame* represents both the internal conflict inside the microcosm and the interpersonal and natural conflict of the outer world.

As always in Beckett, the spectacle is so reduced to the minimum that every single "prop" and costume radiates with special significance. Thus Hamm's handkerchief that he presses to his face reminds us of the cloth with which Veronica wiped the face of Jesus; and Clov's change of clothes connotes a change in his makeup or his intentions. The ash - cans tell us that the contents are considered rubbish.

SIGNIFICANCE OF THE STRUCTURE

Once again, a Beckett play consists ostensibly of a series of little skits and routines. In *Godot* the tramps' improvisations demonstrate the incohesive, diffuse, random qualities of modern life; the master -slave routines of Pozzo - Lucky emphasize the fact that activity provides only the illusion of action. What do the routines mean in *Endgame*? Whenever Hamm and Clov engage in their fierce verbal tilts, each knight (of course, a king is first a knight) seems to take the full brunt of the other's lance; occasionally one seems to us to be "unhorsed" or to think he has unhorsed the other; yet both return to the endless jousting, none the less fierce for its inconclusiveness. Ironically, this knight and this king are on the same "side" in this chess - game! These passages clearly represent the eternal compulsive skirmishing that humanity drives itself to on every level: in internal psychological struggles, in the "rat - race" for "success," in "class warfare," and in the continuous see - saw of international warfare. And whenever Hamm composes a new **episode** in his oral **epic**, it appears to us that he is simply restructuring a part of his own life, to glorify his own ideals, to intensify the conflicts of his past, to justify his own experience and his own attitudes. As a king, of course, he is composing the "chronicles" of his reign. In this effort to impose present meaning on past reality, "technique," manner and plot all seem far more important than real insight into what actually happened. Hence, in spite of their swifter movement (swifter than in *Godot*), and their sustained verbal pyrotechnics, these various routines . . . dialogues and monologues . . . again dramatize the futility and the "bad faith" in which humanity persistently lives.

Also once again, the ending of a Beckett play is ostensibly inconclusive. In *Godot*, we wonder whether Didi will ever . . . on one of these repetitious days . . . crash out of his dream; in *Endgame*, we wonder whether Clov really leaves. Or does he go through this neurotic routine with Hamm every day? Why does Beckett drop the curtain on this tableau? Perhaps to emphasize the importance and/or impossibility of Clov's going. The question is carried away by the audience to be resolved according to each person's own interpretation of the action; and each person's interpretation will depend on the symbolic importance he attributes to Clov and the boy, as we shall see in our discussion of the characterizations.

BROAD IMPLICATIONS IN THE DRAMATIS PERSONAE

Since the five characters . . . four onstage, one sighted offstage . . . clearly represent four generations, it may be worthwhile to consider them in chronological order. As we do that, we are reminded of various cyclical representations of divine and human history. Greek gods, for example, went through a series of "dynasties," representing "progress" from simple concepts like that of an Earth Goddess (Ge) to multiple personifications of natural forces in the Titans to the rule of reason and light in the Olympian gods. Classical writers promulgated myths of the Four Ages of Man, and both classical thinkers like Plato and Renaissance thinkers like Battista Vico formulated theories of the "stages" that a civilization must pass through. These myths and theories are concerned with man's decline from a Golden or Heroic Age of ideal existence, great men, and glorious deeds, down to a mere Brazen Age of petty existence, mean men, and ignominious squabbling. Finally, we are reminded of the way naturalistic writers (like Thomas Mann, *Buddenbrooks*) and others influenced by Theories of Evolution (like Samuel Butler, *The Way of All Flesh*) have considered that four or five generations of characters are the minimum needed for a proper study of the rise and fall of a family or a culture. These considerations in no way interfere with the possibility that four (maybe all five) of the characters in *Endgame* represent parts of the same psyche; all psychoanalytic systems include the "past" as a force in the mind. Freud postulated three forces in the psyche: Ego or social, rational mind; Id, or unconscious, irrational mind; and Super - Ego, a sort of internalized voice of the Authority Figures in the older generations. Jung saw the unconscious mind divided into the personal unconscious and the collective or "racial" unconscious: the latter would give every psyche a complete memory of all the experience of the human race, replete with hallowed, eternal archetypal figures representing human forces like the maternal, paternal, feminine, masculine, and so on. Jung also distinguished between a "true ego" and a "pseudo - ego." A true ego has a creative relationship with the Unconscious; a pseudo - ego has cut itself off from its Unconscious. Pozzo, for example, can be seen as a pseudo - ego that denies the importance of its own racial and spiritual heritage.

NAGG AND NELL

Hamm's parents impress us as representing a tragic paradox we find in so many Authority Figures past and present. Between themselves, Nagg and Nell seem capable of affection, of nostalgic reminiscences, of a kind of communication that ranges from the candid to the coy. They seem as sweet and "romantic" as a tourist's post - card; they seem almost to stand for official virtue and innocence. Yet we infer that as parents they have smugly and sadistically lived according to such traditional precepts as "Children should be seen and not heard." They are types of those parents who feel that humanity includes everybody but the next generation. Nagg reminds us, for example, of that pillar of virtue, the Reverend Theobald Pontifex, who found Sunday afternoon (between his morning and evening services) the best time for thrashing three - year - old Ernest for willfully talking baby - talk (Butler's *The Way of All Flesh*). Closer yet, Nagg's attitude toward Hamm of *Endgame* is reminiscent of Noah's attitude toward Ham in the Bible. After poor Ham had inadvertently seen his father naked, Noah pronounced a solemn patriarchal curse on the boy for what "he had done to him" (Genesis, chapter 9). We are reminded again in Beckett of the arbitrary justice that thunders down through our literature: God's preference for Abel over Cain; Isaac's favoring Esau over Jacob; St. Augustine's emphasis on the fact that one thief was saved, one damned; Theobald and Ernest, etc. Is God's favoritism the main cause of Abel's criminality? Is Isaac's favoritism an explanation of Jacob's cruel code of ethics? Such questions resonate through our mind as we contemplate Hamm's character. Hamm has consigned those sweet old love - birds to the trash heap, and that is a poetic and symbolic revenge, but . . . and this too is beautifully symbolized in the setting as a skull . . . one's progenitors, junked or not, remain part of one's psyche. (The question of the older generation's declaration of war on youth is taken up more explicitly in Beckett's play *All that Fall*.)

HAMM

Certain social scientists believe that no organism can thrive unless it asserts itself aggressively against its environment. Yet society has to curb self - aggrandizement, and humanity - at - large has begun to sense that unless aggression is curbed or ritualized, the race may wipe itself out. Such a predicament is dramatized by the presence of Hamm in the *Endgame* stage of human history. Hamm represents raw power, he seems self - centered, primitive, restlessly experimental, amoral, lusty, lavishly creative and blindly destructive. On the one hand, he symbolizes that part of the unconscious that produces arts like drama and literature; on the other hand, he symbolizes that part of the unconscious that is truculent, arbitrary, self - willed and tyrannical. All these qualities come together in the warlike king who patronizes the arts and loves pageantry. How have such opposites grown together as concomitants in the human personality? How tragic, if true, that in order to curb blind selfishness, we also have to risk crippling our vitality and fecundity! Yet these are the human qualities Hamm seems to comprise on both the social and psychic levels, and it explains our ambivalence towards him. It explains Clov's attitude too. What would Clov be like without Hamm? Hamm seems to be the Life Force itself, the animal part of man. Yet Man could live neither with Hamm nor without him.

What does Hamm . . . enigmatic to the end . . . intend to communicate when he covers his face with a handkerchief? Napoleon could not bear to be crowned by the Pope, to receive his attribute of authority from any except his own hands. And

Hamm must be his own St. Veronica: with his own hands, he declares himself to be the sacrificed King - God. But does he really believe that Clov will leave him (that is, sacrifice him, let him die of neglect)? There are many clues in the play that Hamm and Clov must stay together just as Ego and Id, or mind and body, must somehow get along. Some critics point out that clove is the traditional spice associated with ham. And A. J. Leventhal (in his essay in the Esslin anthology: see Further Reading) suggests that Hamm is an abbreviation for hammer, and that Clov is clou, French for nail; Nell is short for Nello, Italian for nail; and Nagg is short for Nagel, German for nail. Hammer and nails certainly make very little sense without each other. And both Super - Ego (conscience) and Ego (rationality) are in a functional, concomital relationship with the Id (the driving Unconscious force). Recalling that Hamm's name also connotes Noah's arbitrarily punished son, as well as ham actor and Hamlet, we see again that every one of Beckett's names is carefully chosen for its manifold reinforcement of the dramatic situation.

CLOV

In the dynasties of the gods, the progression seemed to be from primitive and irrational forces like Poseidon, lord of the earthquake, to a generation of deities of intellect and harmony, like Athene and Apollo. Yet the trend can go too far. The Kierkegaardian existentialists, as we have seen, expect the intellect - oriented man to collapse into despair as his heart rebels. Jungian psychoanalysts also see disaster for the Ego if it tries to thrive without healthy intercourse with the Unconscious. Beckett himself, in *Waiting for Godot*, portrays a beautiful character, Didi, who cannot realize his own full potential because he refuses the Unconscious its rightful place in life. In his novel *Watt*, Beckett portrays a man whose exclusive passion for rationality actually brings him to a psychotic break.

Clov, representing the third generation in *Endgame*, is closer to Watt than to Didi. In his duties as caretaker of this skull - shelter - Ark, Clov seems so interested in order for its own sake that he reminds us of abstract Platonic forms or Kierkegaard's "shells of truth." Seeming in the tilts to represent Sir Logic, he impresses us too as contemptuous of Hamm's artistic efforts. Worse yet . . . Clov seems equally contemptuous of both the creative and the destructive aspects of Hamm's nature. Tragically, too much of Clov's intellectual talent is channeled into disparagement. While Hamm seems to prey on other forms of life because he is engaged in aggressive struggle for survival, Clov seems to want to exterminate life for sanitary purposes.

CLOV AND THE BOY

All of which makes us apprehensive about the boy Clov has sighted. The child could have a religious significance: we think of the baby Moses, found in the rushes; the babies Romulus and Remus, legendary founders of Rome; and of course, the Christ - Child in the Manger. (Fin de Partie, fuller than the English version *Endgame*, gives the boy definite qualities of a child - Buddha.) All this is significant because worship of a Father God is reverence of the past while worship of a child - god is . . . at least early in his life . . . reverence for the future. Does Clov plan to welcome the boy out there as the new hope, the fourth generation, the future? Much as this seems out of character for Clov, we do recall he is "dressed up" at the end, suggesting a change in his personality, or some festive occasion. But looked at psychoanalytically, as we have noted, the boy could simply represent the new Self - Image that is emerging in this skull.

Clov in that case is preparing to carry out his duties as the Ego, or caretaker of this psychic complex, which has perceived the possibility of this new Self and is now coming to terms with it. Or... again not unrelatedly... the boy can simply symbolize the outer world. Clov, tied down all this time in internal, subjective conflicts, is finally turning outward toward the Macrocosm which for him is fresh and unknown and offers young opportunities. This introvert psyche that comprises Clov - Hamm - Nagg - Nell may now... under Clov's direction... become more extrovert.

CLOV, THE BOY, AND THE FUTURE

Endgame, then, through its spectacle, its structure, and its characterization, says that man is in a critical transition. If he ends his suicidal internal conflict between his Conscious and his Unconscious; if he resolves the petty power - squabbles in which he dissipates his energies; he may yet rally and create a new Self, a new Species. (Nietzsche said man is something that must be surpassed.) But who can win a chess -game with so few pieces in such an endgame situation? Beckett hasn't closed the door there either. That boy is far away from this corner of the chess - board where the king and his lone knight and his two other, pinned - down pieces are trapped. Is that boy a pawn who has made it all away across the board and thus is (with the knight's sudden help) about to become the most powerful piece, a queen? One way or another, the next move is Mankind's, acting in unison with all its resources, or else....

LANGUAGE IN ENDGAME

Beckett's talent for stichomythy figures in *Endgame* too. As a matter of fact, it is the rapid and regular exchange of language between Hamm and Clov that makes *Endgame* a swiftly - moving play. And the superb cadence and vocalizing that helped make *Godot* almost a verse drama have been developed in *Endgame* to near perfection. We tend to think that music is the only art medium in which form and content are identical. With *Endgame*, Beckett almost brings dialogue to that level; Beckett's use of language here is so utterly under control that the sounds of words and their meanings almost seem inseparable, as though English were totally onomatopoetic. The puns are more functional and more ironical than in *Godot*, ranging all the way from quibbles over English grammar (p.34) and a neat joke over the power of the telescope (p. 29) to brilliant word - plays on existentialism (pp. 49, 74). One would be hard - put to try to pick the better play on the basis of writing style because *Godot* has lyrical passages that *Endgame* does not try to emulate. But Beckett said something interesting about *Endgame* which sums up both his intention and his effect. In a letter to Alan Schneider, describing *Endgame*, Beckett spoke about the "power of the language to claw."

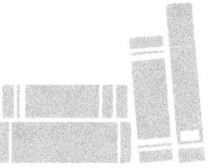

OTHER PLAYS

KRAPP'S LAST TAPE

HISTORY

A technical tour de force and probably the most famous of Beckett's shorter plays, *Krapp's Last Tape* was written directly into English soon after Beckett completed *Endgame* in 1957. It was first performed at the Royal Court Theater in London, on October 28, 1958, on the same bill with *Endgame*. Frequently produced in Europe, it became the sensation of the off-Broadway season when it opened in the Provincetown Playhouse in Greenwich Village early in 1960. That same year *Krapp's Last Tape* was issued by Grove Press as a "quality" paperback that includes four other short pieces by Beckett.

NATURE OF THE SITUATION

In this play, Beckett uses an ingenious device for dramatizing man's difficulty in establishing a continuous identity across time. In order to discuss the dramaturgic and thematic achievements of the play, we should first remind ourselves of these crucial elements in the action:

Krapp, 69, an alcoholic writer, plays a tape made on his thirty-ninth birthday. The younger Krapp describes his last time with a woman he rejected; he scoffs at a tape made earlier which discussed his drinking problem. The older Krapp, skipping intellectual passages, plays the "39" tape twice; tries to record a "69" tape; disparages the younger Krapp; and desperately goes back to replay that love scene.

CRITIQUE

With this play, Beckett became the first dramatist to use tape-recording as a means of staging a man's confrontation with one of his own selves! This exciting device has the additional advantage of emphasizing spectacle, an element of drama in which Beckett excels. For most of the play, we simply watch the current Krapp as he responds to the younger Krapp. Even to us, there are similarities, yet "69" often seems to react to "39" as he would to a total stranger, and in the end, we gather that "69" hates "39" as he would a rival or even an enemy. This technique is even more remarkable if we add to what we have already noted the fact that Beckett has given us here a new twist on the play-within-a-play. It is always suspenseful to watch a character who is watching a play: for example, in *Hamlet*, we watch King Claudius (suspected of murdering the ex-king in order to gain his wife and throne) as he watches a play, staged by Prince Hamlet, in which a king is murdered by his wife's lover, etc. The "dramatic pleasure" here consists in the fact that dramatic **irony** has been compounded. Ordinarily we watch a character act out his life in partial ignorance of crucial facts already known to the audience. Hence the double **irony** of the play-within-a-play: we know more about the larger situation than Hamlet does;

we watch how he acts as he knows more about the immediate situation than the king does; but the king and we know things that Hamlet doesn't. The play - within - a - play teaches us, more than any other single artistic device, how fragile, how relative, how vain all human knowledge is. See how Beckett uses the device. Of course, the audience knows more about "69" than "39" does. Then we hear the voice of- "39" speaking in pathetic ignorance of what he will later become, and we watch the effect of these revelations of ignorance on "69" (who after all contains another version of "39" inside his present Self!). Beckett lays overlay on overlay, for "39" laughs at a tape made by an even younger Krapp; and we ourselves become acutely reminded that others watch us strut in our ignorance (of ourselves especially).

The resolution of the play grows superbly out of this central **irony**. At 39, Krapp could reject a lover not knowing he would never again have such a chance for happiness; at 69 he wants to play that last love - scene over and over; he needs to hear now those words of tenderness, that sexual dialogue, but then he has to pay the price of hearing too the evidence of his own cruel, arrogant blindness.

In its plot, *Krapp's Last Tape* is a compact statement of man's predicament as a prisoner of Time. Unwittingly, he preserves the worst in himself (largely through habit) and throws the best away. In its technique, *Tape* reminds us of the Heraclitean disenchantment extended in our time to the subjective investigation. Krapp is investigating himself. But his research is invalidated by the fact that Krapp - the -investigator and Krapp - the - investigated have both changed. Man has to go on doing the impossible: patching together a character, a Self, made up out of bits of then and now!

GODOT, ENDGAME, AND KRAPP

Krapp's Last Tape continues an inquiry into man's nature begun as early as Beckett's essay on Proust. In that work, Beckett stresses the way habit stifles spontaneity, the way man struggles to preserve an identity in the stream of time. In the early novels, Beckett explored first man's division into contemplative and active selves (Murphy), then his division into rational and irrational selves (*Watt*). In dramatizing man's self-dichotomizing in *Godot* and *Endgame*, Beckett found it necessary to personify each of the divisive forces (Gogo and Hamm as different types of Id, Didi and Clov as different types of Ego). In *Krapp's Last Tape* he found, through advances in electronics, a perfect medium for dramatizing man's internal conflict while presenting that man in his ultimate **irony** . . . that is, as a physical unity.

KRAPP AS SCIENCE FICTION

Krapp has some claim to being a science-fiction play. Since no one in 1957 could have in his possession any tapes of his own voice in 1927, the play was obviously set in the future. Briefly, Beckett was paralleling the work of "s-f" writers concerned with how man can meet himself across time.

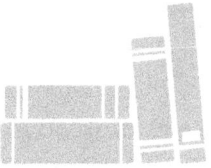

OTHER PLAYS

ALL THAT FALL

....

First presented by the British Broadcasting Corporation's Third Programme on January 13, 1957, *All that Fall: A Play for Radio* is important for the student of Beckett for several reasons: (1) It throws light on the symbolism and possible fate of the boy in *Endgame* and maybe even in *Godot*. In this radio play, an elderly man, coming home on a commuter train, throws a child out of a train - window to its death on the tracks. If, in *Endgame* and *Godot* the child signifies the possibility of a new Self, here we have another clear indication of why Gogo is so angry at the goat - boy and how Clov is likely to treat that boy -god outside. We also have another clear proof of Beckett's conviction that the older generation (as represented by Nagg and Nell) can be barbaric in its treatment of the young. (2) In *All that Fall*, Beckett makes his usual divisions of the psyche along unusual lines; that is, as sexual differences. The elderly man seems to be Beckett's coldly logical and mathematical Ego, while his wife represents the emotional, creative Id. Usually Beckett does not see psychic differences as sexual in nature, probably because (as Saroyan suggests: See Review Of Criticism), Beckett feels these psychic forces are to be found (or not found) in either sex. In *All that Fall*, the psychic differences are distributed more as Virginia

Woolf distributes them in *To the Lighthouse* and *Mrs. Dalloway*. (3) The *Godot* **themes** are reinforced in all that Fall. Once again we have blindness, sterility, physical infirmity used as symbols of the condition of the human race; active and passive states contrasted; and terribly bruising **episodes** about the effect of machines on man. (4) For Beckett, there is in *All that Fall* an unusual reliance on the traditional technique of revelation. Beckett resolves this play as Arthur Miller would resolve it: simply by having a vital piece of information withheld until the end. (5) *All that Fall,* written expressly for radio, shows Beckett's amazing ability to adapt to the medium. Through sound alone, he communicates all his desired effects like a veteran radio - writer. (6) This play demonstrates how great British writers like Beckett (Dylan Thomas, et al.) could go on writing for radio long after radio - drama had been all but abandoned in the United States (in spite of the impressive works for the medium by Archibald MacLeish, Norman Corwin, et al.).

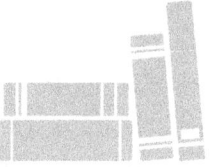

THREE NOVELS

MOLLOY, MALONE DIES, THE UNNAMABLE

HISTORY OF THREE NOVELS

Beckett's most famous work of fiction was composed in French during the late 1940's, when he was enjoying a phenomenal burst of creativity in both fictional and dramatic media. The first two novels . . . *Molloy* and *Malone Meurt* . . . were published in Paris in 1951; the third, L'Innommable, in 1953. English translations, prepared by Patrick Bowles in close collaboration with Beckett, were published in New York by Grove Press (*Molloy* in 1955; *Malone Dies*, 1956; The *Unnamable*, 1958) and later issued in a one - volume edition as *Three Novels*.

Molloy was hailed by French critics as a major event. The work was discussed and exegesed in learned journals and avant - garde periodicals. Typical of the praise heaped on Beckett is Maurice Nadeau's remark in Mercure de France (August 1951) that "*Molloy*, the first of his works really to register, establishes him at once among the great." (Nadeau's review is reprinted in the Esslin anthology: see Further Reading.) Hence it was Beckett's trilogy that established him in the art world before

Godot made him known to the general public. Today, the trilogy has caused novelist Beckett to be ranked along with Kafka and Joyce much as *Godot* has caused dramatist Beckett to be discussed along with Pirandello and Brecht.

THREE NOVELS AS A QUEST

All written in the first person, the three novels represent three phases of one individual's quest for his own identity. Like Krapp in *Krapp's Last Tape*, like Hamm in *Endgame*, this individual is using a verbal medium to sift his own memories in an effort to discover whether he has actually lived. Like Krapp, like Hamm, this man of many selves (hence unnamable) finds no proof of any genuine achievement. Beckett does not intend to disparage only the "I" of his trilogy; like the "I" in Whitman's poetry, the first-person in Beckett's trilogy is intended to represent Everyman, the "hypocrite reader," as well as the hero and the author too. The "I" discovers that not only he, but all humanity, has wasted its chance.

To discuss the symbolism and the **themes** of the trilogy, as well as its relation to *Godot*, we need to remind ourselves first of these crucial facts about the quest:

Molloy, suffering from progressive paralysis, now rides a bicycle, now crutches, in a long and half - hearted search now for his mother, then for his father. Obsessed with his hat, carrying pebbles as his vade mecums, he becomes so lost that some Authority Figure sends an investigator, Moran, to hunt Molloy; by the end of his first novel, Molloy and Moran have had so many similar experiences they have become almost identical. In the second novel, the "I" now thinks of himself as Malone; bedridden, he writes his memoirs. Approaching death raises an ironical question: Who is it, exactly, that is dying? Sometimes Malone thinks it is Lambert, or Sapsocat, or Macmann who is in love with Moll. By the third novel, the "I" has become almost entirely a solipsist; he believes himself sometimes to be Mahood, a paraplegic stuck like a sprig of flowers in a jar; sometimes the Worm; other times the creator not only of *Molloy* and *Malone* but also of *Watt* and *Mercier*. The trilogy ends with *the Unnamable* having somehow to reconcile his personal disgust over his lack of identity with his human obligation to go on living anyhow.

CHARACTERIZATION

Each figure that appears as a separate character in *Three Novels* is really a part . . . or a temporary combination of parts . . . of one total (hence chaotic) psyche. Molloy, for example, can be experienced as the Id that vaguely hopes to return to the womb (hence the search for the mother); Moran is felt to be the fussy Ego engaged in a search for its basis in Molloy. The closer these two get to each other, the more they fade as separate parts, the more they overlap and blend. Neither these nor any other "characters" can be sure of their own experience because they cannot really separate dream from reality, sleeping from waking life, fantasy from objective history. And so we do not know whether Macmann, in love with Moll, is a memory of an earlier "real" experience of Malone's (like Krapp's one love affair) or is one of his present fantasies. Like H. C. Earwicker of Joyce's *Finnegans Wake*, *Molloy - Malone - Unnamable* thinks at times out of his deepest "racial" unconscious. Thus Molloy seems often to be Homer's Odysseus, encountering on his travels people who remind us of Proteus, Circe, Nausicaa, but acting toward each of them in an ironical or "Freudian" way: for example, is "Circe" really Molloy's mother whom he has failed to recognize? Or does he dream of his mother disguised as Circe or Calypso? The very name Molloy, in this context, conjures up Hermes, Greek god of speed, patron of thieves, guardian of highways and travel, whose attributes were the traveler's hat and the root moly. Moly, we recall, protected Odysseus from Circe, and Greeks generally from the lunar magic of the dark goddess Hecate. Furthermore, Hermes was supposed to be able to read the future from arrangements of stones! Of course, when we think of Molloy as thinking of himself as Hermes, we experience an ironic contrast because Molloy is anything but speedy: even riding his bicycle, he is still stiff - legged, senile, struggling with crutches. He is a pathetic descendant of the wing - footed god.

In his racial unconscious, the "I" of the trilogy is also Hebraic - Christian as well as Greek. In some scenes Molloy - Moran's bicycle strikes us as the ass on which the King rides into Jerusalem. The "I's" agonizing journey is like a calvary, a painful struggle up to a crucifixion, with the crutches as the cross, each stop a "station." Always we sense reminders of sheep, two thieves, two or three crosses. And the Authority Figure that sends Moran hunting for Molloy is a Father - God, a Jehovah - like patriarch. Molloy's pebbles are also as Biblical as they are Hellenic: we think not only of David's choosing his stones for his slingshot, but also of the insinuating cry in the Sermon on the Mount: Is there a man among you who will offer his son a stone when he asks for bread . .? (Matthew, chapter 9). Yes, life supplies Molloy most generously . . . with pebbles. And the only Goliath he ever topples is himself.

When the Unnamable floats back and forth from existence as Mahood to existence as Worm, he is still vaguely engaged in a search for identity in his mother (Ma - hood, motherhood) and in his father (Worm is a classic Freudian symbol both for phallus and sperm). Again, when the Unnamable exists as Mahood, the paraplegic in a jar, he is also the innermost mind sealed deep inside the body. This is the pure "vegetable" existence of the "I", for Mahood is cared for like flowers in a vase. And when the Unnamable thinks of all the characters he has been, created, personified, objectified, lived with, he is thinking like Beckett. (After all, Watt is a character from another work, and Mercier is a character from an unpublished novel!) But of course the psychoanalyst tells us that artistic creations must be regarded and interpreted as dreams. So some of Beckett's characters are like the many selves that Everyman creates in his reveries, his nightmares, his frantic search for self - justification and the perfect rationalization; some are like the many other selves that simply emerge unbidden from the unconscious, for example, the sudden angry self that commits outrage before the Ego can stop it. Everyman's Ego might afterward use its logical powers to "rationalize" what the Id has done, but the Unnamable at the end can no longer rationalize; his self -inventory has put him in the balance and found him wanting. Wanting mainly because he can never assemble all the parts into one co - ordinated Self.

STYLE OF THREE NOVELS

The reader of Beckett's plays, accustomed to sparse statements, the "reductive" language of *Godot* and *Endgame*, is delighted with the contrast he meets in *Three Novels*. For here Beckett, unable to use stage spectacle or radio sound - effects, explores instead all of the resources of pure "writing," and he acquits himself as superbly in fictional as in dramatic composition. Basically simple and lucid (for the reader who relaxes, that is, and allows the language to work suggestively on him), Beckett's prose rises to any occasion. He creates a different style for each "I": we go abruptly from Molloy's conscientious rambling to Moran's fussy pertinacity. And Beckett reaches us subliminally as well as on the rational level. For example, while seemingly narrating events in an unidentified country, Beckett ... we suddenly realize ... has created in us the impression we have been among the Canaan hills, in a medieval town, or on an Aegean beach ... he has struck all these chords in our memories of Biblical narrative, Arthurian romance, Homeric **epic**. He impresses us too as far superior to that master of parody, Joyce. With consummate and seemingly effortless skill, Beckett reproduces the patterns of intellectual "pursuit," rationalization, self -analysis, even the meaningful babble of reverie. One of his basic literary devices is the sentence that negates itself, as for example, a sentence of interior monologue that builds up to an absolute certainty and then very innocently qualifies itself and qualifies itself until the "build - up" has become a "let - down." This technique produces many charming examples not only of anti - **climax**, but also of oxymoron and epigram. Perhaps most important is the way Beckett makes the prose include the problems of writing itself. By hunting for the word or phrases he needs, the "I" shows that life is not a result but a process.

PARALLELS BETWEEN PLAYS AND NOVELS

We have deliberately emphasized here those symbols and problems in Three Novels that parallel the manner and matter of *Godot* and *Endgame*. The *Three Novels*, obviously, constitute a much fuller, more detailed explanation of many **themes** so starkly presented in the plays. The student soon realizes that Beckett's works are so complementary that they reinforce, ramify, and explain each other.

In all his works, Beckett sees Mankind as in a state of senility and physical disability, tired, self -divided, self - stultifying. Man takes to machines, and he uses tools as crutches, partly to replace his dying physique with more reliable, more durable extensions.

But he still has an animal nature with which he must get along; the struggle for co - existence between his body and his mind is mutually enervating. While the body defects, the mind itself is a battleground of forces rational and irrational, contemplative and active, habitual and spontaneous. There are internalized voices of conscience, spiritual forces hopelessly yearning for recognition, inchoate unconscious energies that must be allowed to create or suffered to destroy. The Ego cannot cope with this inner chaos because most of its energies are channeled outward, either by Society's demands or by the Ego's own flight from itself. As a consequence, the modern Ego is cold, sterile, cut off from its own inner sources of power; and so those unconscious powers, untapped, stagnate. But Man's one hope is that the Ego will learn how to explore Inner Space, how to recouple the dissociated parts of the psyche, re - unify human nature. *Godot* is within. The new Self that could be created may be symbolized or externalized as a babe "out there" but he has to be reckoned with . . . either nurtured or murdered . . . inside Man.

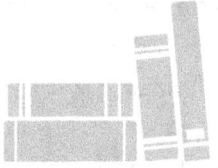

ESSAY QUESTIONS AND ANSWERS

....

Question: What significance do you see in the fact that there are no women in the cast of *Waiting for Godot*?

Answer: One could maintain that Beckett uses only male characters because he is talking about male problems in a man's world. Granted, in our patriarchal society both God, the priest, and the "slave - driver" are masculine in gender. Hence *Godot*, the goat - herd priest, and Pozzo would have to be male to be truly representative. One could even go so far as William Saroyan goes when he suggests that in using only male characters, Beckett might mean that waiting is more characteristic of men than of women. Maybe it is true, given our traditions and opportunities, that men are more concerned with long - range possibilities and women more with immediacy. And this could all add up to an inference that Beckett is blaming men and "male supremacy" for what he regards as the world's "mess."

Nevertheless, I prefer to defend the view that Beckett uses an all - male cast mainly for other reasons. I believe he wants his characters to be sexually neutral, and hence representative of neither men or women but of humanity - at - large. Also, the presence of both sexes on stage always suggests excitement and fertility, whereas the effect that Beckett obviously wants in this play is one of stagnation and sterility.

On one level, at least, Beckett seems interested in using each character to represent one force in the human psyche. For example, Gogo can be seen as representing emotionality, physicality; Didi as human reason; Pozzo as the need for power; Lucky as the need for protection. If Beckett had distributed these forces in the psyche among male and female characters, he might have been suggesting that some of these traits are basically sexual in nature. Actually, he seems to believe that any human characteristic can be found (or not found) in either sex. Each male character in *Waiting for Godot*, as I see it, stands not for maleness but for humanness.

As example of the effect of distributing human characteristics so they seem to be sexual traits can be found in the way Virginia Woolf assigns earthiness and convivial sympathy to female characters (like Mrs. Ramsay) and rationalism and judgmentalism to male characters (like Professor Ramsay, in *To the Lighthouse*). One consequences is that we feel that Mrs. Woolf believes that men are inherently more concerned with logic, that women are inherently more humane. Rarely, to my knowledge, does Beckett divide traits along strictly sexual lines. In his *All that Fall*, Mr. Rooney is cold, mathematical, categorizing in his attitudes toward life, while Mrs. Rooney is the champion of feeling and impulse. While this is more traditional, it is not typical of Beckett, who seems (to me at least) to feel that psychic differences within either sex are greater than psychic differences between sexes.

With only men on stage waiting for the word from a Father Figure; with complete absence of the child - bearing sex, we have humanity as its most static in *Waiting for Godot*. By dramatic contrast, this is poignantly emphasized in that scene in which all the men fall down and embrace Mother Earth.

Question: Beckett is often referred to as a philosophical writer. What evidence do you see in *Waiting for Godot* of his philosophical interests?

Answer: Beckett seems to be interested in most philosophies for the way they reflect or affect human behavior; only one of the major philosophical systems that figure in his work does he treat in any sympathetic way. For example, Heraclitus' "Everything flows" is used as the basis for a bitter pun, and Berkeley's esse est percipi is apparently lampooned in at least one pantomime routine; theological speculation is implicitly condemned for its procrastination and obfuscation; positivism and rationalism are implicitly arraigned for leading man into faith in verbal and mathematical reasoning. But the two philosophical systems that figure most extensively and artistically in *Godot* are the Cartesian and the Kierkegaardian, and only the latter is represented in a positive fashion.

Descartes, whose biography and speculation seem to contribute much to Beckett's subject - matter, is most famous for his starting point of Zero. Supposedly, he reasoned away all cherished beliefs except his conviction that he was thinking. Cogito ergo sum, he concluded: I think, therefore I am. This basic Cartesian concept is satirized throughout Beckett and especially in *Godot*. Didi and Gogo have arrived at a starting point of Zero and it proves to be a launching pad for nowhere. Didi, Gogo, and Lucky all think and therefore they are . . . miserable. For Didi, cogito means "I reason purely, with no references to dreams." This is ironic because Didi's supposedly rational faith proves to be pure rationalization of cherished illusion. Ironic too because Didi's cogitation always brings him round a full 360 degrees. For Gogo, cogito means "I muse, I pun, I criticize." For Lucky, cogito means "I keep my mouth shut until Pozzo says, 'Think, pig!'"

"Think" means different things for different people. And each of these types of thinking . . . which we could label, respectively, logical, organized thought; random, visual mental activity; and "brainstorming," or free association under pressure . . . has its value in human pursuits. Unfortunately, each by itself, unsupported by the others, is ineffective. This is one of Beckett's main themes: man's inability to coordinate all his psychic resources for constructive purposes is part of his tragedy.

Descartes appears in other ways in *Godot*. He believed that all shapes and motions can be apprehended through geometry. Calisthenics and other, vaudeville - like routines that Didi and Gogo endure while waiting, and automatic movements that Lucky makes on command, seem to be **satires** of this Cartesian concept. Lucky's mechanical motions also illustrate other notions of Descartes: he conceived of man's body as a machine; and in an interesting adumbration of cybernetics, he discusses a machine that would produce human responses. The way Pozzo has Lucky programmed to act mechanically is a take -off on these cogitations about man - as - machine and man - as - user- of- machines.

Kierkegaard, Sartre, and other existentialists seem to be reflected most sympathetically in Beckett. Kierkegaard said that any abstract "truth" about the nature of the world, precisely because it has been abstracted from human experiences, dies and becomes a mere "shell of truth." There can be no truth separate from human activity. To Kierkegaard, then, subjectivity is prior to objectivity; becoming (existence) is of a higher reality than being (essence). Kierkegaard considers the psychological effect on man of the fact that through his intellect, he deals so much with generalizations, abstractions, "essences." All the rest of his nature yearns for real experience, for existence. This struggle between mind and heart leads to a crisis. Man becomes paralyzed by dread, anxiety (Angst) ... because if he breaks out of his mind - limited, objectivist way of life, the possibilities are infinite, and nothing is certain. Man tends to hover in this area of uncertainty. Yet in all such crises, says Kierkegaard, man must act decisively. "Choice" is the most precious thing granted to man.

Contemporary existentialists disagree on whether God, as perfect essence, is dead, a "shell of truth." But Sartre says that whether God exists is irrelevant; to be manly, man must act as if there is no God in any event. He cannot be manly if he looks outside himself for guidance, salvation, justification. "We are alone." Sartre's view of choice is that one way or another, man always chooses himself. Even when he thinks he is not choosing, he is still choosing.

Waiting for Godot clearly offers an existentialist view of man's condition. Didi and Gogo yearn for real existence, yet they look outside themselves for salvation, they look toward some abstract truth. Didi is "mind," afraid of the rebellion of his own "heart" (Gogo), yet afraid too to break out of this trap, to be on his own, alone in a Universe without Godot, with only Nothing. So he falls back into his delusion that his center of gravity is outside himself. This seems to sum up the philosophical message of *Waiting for Godot*: Man, unable to coordinate his psychic resources, keeps vigil for Godot; but Godot waits inside man to be discovered.

Question: In what specific ways does *Waiting for Godot* deviate from traditional theater?

Answer: *Waiting for Godot* deviates from traditional theater in spectacle, structure, and characterization. Beckett does not use a realistic setting or realistic properties. Rather he uses a symbolic setting, with a tree that has religious implications, a road that seems to suggest time and travel. The "props" too are symbolic: a hat for Didi to fuss with because he is "mental" in his orientation, boots for Gogo to worry about because he is more earthy, a whip for Pozzo the master, a "leash" for his slave. But stage movements are important too: Lucky moves like an automaton, the tramps go through little routines, all to suggest man's reduction of his body to mere mechanical and habitual functions.

In structure *Waiting for Godot* violates all traditional expectations, all the prescriptions of Aristotle, Freytag, Egri. There is no rising action, no converging of all awareness on a crisis, no traditional catharsis with its purgation of emotions and its enlightenment. Rather, the action emphasizes the monotony, the unremitting tedium, the aimlessness, the cyclical nature of man's existence.

Beckett also disappoints the playgoer who expects traditional characterization, with its positivist motivation, its critical growth or development, its insights. Gogo and Didi do not seem to change at all; Didi has a brief brush with an opportunity to break out of his condition but cannot summon up the strength. Pozzo and Lucky change drastically, but apparently without any "causation" other than Time and Fate. Overtly, there is little conflict in the usual sense; there are no crucial confrontations because Didi and Gogo are waiting for someone who never comes and Pozzo and Lucky are just passing through. It would be contrary to Beckett's aim to present sharp, clear - cut, meaningful conflict, growth, or insight. He aims to show that man has worked himself into a dark thicket of self - contradictions in which he is immobilized. The one and only insight that would save him . . . that he must be his own Godot . . . is the one he spends all his time avoiding.

Question: What does Godot represent? Who is waiting for him, and why?

Answer: All that we can say, from our experience of the play, is that Godot is that ideal power outside Didi which Didi believes will solve his and Gogo's problems. Beyond that, how each playgoer interprets Godot is likely to depend on how much history and psychology he knows, how he defines religion and God, and how he himself feels about the human condition. For Godot can be seen as a traditional Deity whose Second Coming is awaited by man; or as an Ideal Prince who has promised an Utopian State; or as any force, any bolt out of the blue, that mankind looks to for salvation and that hence prevents man from taking his destiny in his own hands.

That religion is the force that Beckett has in mind could be inferred from the fact that much of the dialogue, spectacle, and symbolism reflect traditional Hebraic and Christian values. The single tree on stage suggest, the Tree of Knowledge, the "tree" on which Jesus was crucified, the tree on which Judas hanged himself. Knowledge is exactly what Didi and Gogo are yearning for, vaguely; they experience the kind of spiritual agony we have come to describe as "calvary;" and they contemplate suicide. But what most of all suggests that Godot is God is that he sends a messenger: that is, the tramps make contact with Godot only through an intermediary, who must thus be seen as a priest - figure. This intermediary is a goat - herd. Since Jesus was a shepherd, since he threatened to separate the sheep from the goats, and since followers of the pagan god Pan thought of him as half - goat, half man, we find here many ironical **allusions** to man's conception of godhead. It is significant too that Pozzo, who owns all the surrounding land, seems to live in total ignorance of Godot. Godot seems to exist only in the minds of his followers. If Godot is a Deity, then the play says that man is waiting for a god who is either dead, has abandoned his flock, or is strictly a human concept.

A Jungian critic has seen special significance in Godot's timing. Dr. Eva Metman points out that Godot's messenger arrives just in time to prevent any chance Didi might reach full - awareness. She believes Godot has a vested interest in keeping his believers off - balance, that he does not want them to free themselves of their dependence on him. Is Godot then some force in society that wants man to endure his suffering now because of some illusory reward later?

Because Didi and Gogo are landless, poor, and migratory, and because Didi is indignant at the exploitation of the weak and seems concerned about the way of life that Godot provides for his people, we could see Godot as some great social leader who promises liberation for the oppressed. Some critics have also suggested that Godot resembles Aristotle's Unmoved Mover, who moves the Universe the way the beloved moves the lover. Others believe that Godot has actually appeared on stage in disguise . . . either as Pozzo, or the goatherd, or Lucky, or maybe even Gogo himself. All of these seem to be ramifications of . . . and best included in . . . the only definite assumption the play allows us to make:

Godot is Man's Hope, which he mistakenly believes is outside himself.

Question: What do the four main characters in *Waiting for Godot* seem to represent?

Answer: I must emphasize that the four main characters first of all represent themselves. If they could not do that in a convincing manner, they would have no artistic existence and so would not be able to represent anything beyond themselves. Most of all, then, Didi is a man who is "patient as Job," with human failings, a touching faith in rationality, a terror of the irrational, a man as self - honest as he can be if he is to maintain his basic illusions. Gogo is a person more concerned with the physical and emotional, but to such an extent that he is diffuse and needs whatever focus his more rational - minded friend Didi can provide. Pozzo is cynical, pragmatic, materialistic; he has no powers of personal growth, and so when he is hit with disaster, he can only be embittered with Time. Lucky is educated and cultured, but so without a will of his own that he is uncritically dependent on Pozzo for direction and sustenance.

Beyond what they are as stage personalities, what do these four characters represent? All artistic creations must also have some representative value: their appeal would be minuscule without it.

Pozzo and Lucky dramatize the futility of seeking fulfillment in the material world. Pozzo, through his own will, drives himself and others in the fierce activity of gaining power over people and possessions. Lucky, because he lacks will and economic security, participates in this frantic race. Lucky seems intellectual by nature, but his real talents are wasted because a world run by Pozzo is a world in which only things count. In violating his own nature for the mere leavings of the master's table, in adjusting to Pozzo's system, Lucky has himself become a thing. The Pozzo - Lucky world has its historical analogies not only in such power - systems as the Roman Empire, but even in the two major power - systems today, both of which are basically materialistic in their values.

Didi and Gogo, seen as individuals, seem to represent the rational and irrational forces, respectively, in man. Taken as a pair, they dramatize the futility of waiting for fulfillment in some ideal world. If Pozzo and Lucky are seen as locked in internecine economic conflict, then Didi and Gogo can represent mankind engaged in paralyzing psychological conflict. Exhausted and stultified by their neurotic interplay, they are waiting for a saviour, a rescuer. They too represent strong historical forces. Through the ages, mankind has waited for a saviour.

Both these approaches . . . the Pozzo - Lucky search in the material world and the Gogo - Didi search in an ideal world . . . have one thing in common. In both cases, the goal, the yearned - for reality, is located outside the Self. Gogo, who seems to represent the Id, senses there is a universe inside himself worth exploring; but Didi, who represents the Ego, is terrified of the Id and succeeds in suppressing its influence in their relationship. And Lucky is prevented by his materialistic master from following his own intellectual bent.

Idealism, that is, dualism with belief in a second world of values higher than this world; and materialism, or the belief that there is nothing but this world, both these approaches fail in *Waiting for Godot*. The possibility of a third approach shapes up briefly in Didi's famous soliloquy. He comes close to seeing that Godot can be found in himself. Although Didi shrinks back, it seems clear . . . to me at least . . . that Beckett is saying that that third approach is the only one man has not really tried and yet the only one he really needs.

Question: In the total dramatic effect achieved by *Waiting for Godot*, what part does language play? For example, how does Beckett's language relate to his **themes** and his characterization?

Answer: Beckett's language . . . like his spectacle and his structure . . . reinforces and ramifies his **themes** and his characterization.

Again and again, the dialogue in *Waiting for Godot* demonstrates that communication is tenuous; reasoning is cyclical; certainty is impossible. Lyricism leads to obscurantism. Language in *Godot* proves to be just as much a "routine" as the pantomimes. It is more likely to perpetuate whatever neurosis and habit are already there than to lead to any clarification. Beckett's language, in short, proves his themes.

In *Waiting for Godot* language also helps create and differentiate the characters. When we remember Didi's speech, we remember that it is he who tries to explore a problem fully in words; it is Didi who is more concerned with finding the right word, who will attempt an epigram, who will re - state Hamlet's dilemma (To be or not to be, that is the question) in parallel language that precisely defines the difference in the **themes** of the two plays. And it is Didi who strains toward self - realization by posing questions about his condition. Didi's speech, from the most casual to the most anguished, is the speech of a man using language to struggle for intellectual insight. But when we remember Gogo's speech, we recall that he is more likely to proceed not by logic but by free association; it is Gogo who will invoke an euphemism, a proverb, a Heraclitean precept mainly as the basis for a pun or a parody. His language is less directed, more anarchic. We recall that it is in Gogo's voice we have heard both the more violent and the more naively poignant feelings expressed. Gogo's language is the language of acceptance, acceptance even of obscurity.

Just as Beckett creates a separate language for each of the two tramps, so does he create a language to express their feelings as a couple. When they cease their bickering and function in concert, their languages blend into one. They match each other's ideas, word for word, phrase for phrase, in spontaneous parallelism, as they use language to express the quality of a mutual experience. In these "duets," as they deserve to be called, Beckett uses a kind of stichomythy, or a rapid series of short statements that balance each other musically. As a matter of fact, it is in these stichomythic passages that we can best study Beckett's control over the music of speech. In these passages he employs **alliteration**, half - **rhymes** (especially dissonance), and feminine endings. After discovering the deliberate artistry in Beckett's stichomythy, we are prepared to notice in detail how even his long speeches are precisely vocalized and cadenced.

Pozzo and Lucky, as Beckett conceived them, required almost bizarre language. Again, we recall them as unique because of their unique speech. We remember Pozzo as the man who affects lyrical sentiments or actually builds up, in the middle of a roadside chat, to a formal presentation. He glibly uses language for special effects, as do advertisers, salesmen, and demagogues. But after his great metamorphosis, he can no longer play on language as on an instrument; now language rather emerges involuntarily from him like the cries of a wounded animal. And of course, when we remember Lucky, we remember that tirade, that oracular diatribe, that spate of gibberish that expresses in distorted and distilled language all that poor Lucky has had to suppress.

In creating a special language for each character, and in making all their speeches reinforce the **themes** of his play, Beckett has demonstrated absolute mastery over a great range of literary devices.

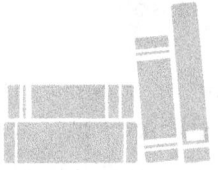

BIBLIOGRAPHY

PRIMARY SOURCES

Beckett, Samuel. *Collected Works.* Sixteen volumes. New York: Grove Press, 1970.

____. *Waiting for Godot.* New York: Grove Press, 1954.

____. *Endgame.* New York: Grove Press, 1958.

____. *Krapp's Last Tape and Other Dramatic Pieces.* New York: Grove Press, 1958.

____. *Three Novels: Molloy, Malone Dies, The Unnamable.* New York: Grove Press, 1955.

____. *More Pricks than Kicks.* London: Chatto and Windus, 1934. New York: Grove Press, 1970.

____. *How it is.* New York: Grove Press, 1964.

____. *Watt.* New York: Grove Press, 1959.

____. *Stories and Texts for Nothing.* New York: Grove Press, 1967.

SECONDARY SOURCES

Anonymous. *Review of Waiting for Godot*. Times Literary Supplement. February 10, 1956.

Bakewell, Michael. "Working with Beckett." *Adam: A Literary Quarterly in English and French.* Vol. 35, Nos. 337-339, 1970.

Calder, John. "Beckett... Man and Artist." *Adam.* Vol. 35, Nos. 337-339, 1970.

Chevigny, Bell Gale, editor. *Endgame: A Collection of Critical Essays*. Englewood Cliffs, N.J.: Prentice - Hall, 1969.

Clayes, Stanley, editor. *Drama and Discussion*. New York: Meredith Publishing, 1967.

Cohn, Ruby, editor. *Casebook on Waiting for Godot*. New York: Grove Press, 1967.

____. *Samuel Beckett: The Comic Gamut*. New Brunswick, N.J.: Rutgers University Press, 1962.

Dobree, Bonamy. "The London Theatre, 1957." *Sewanee Review.* Vol. LXVI, Winter 1958.

Driver, Tom F. "Beckett by the Madeleine." *Columbia University Forum.* Volume IV, Summer 1961.

____. *Romantic Quest and Modern Query*. New York: Delacorte, 1970.

Esslin, Martin, editor. *Samuel Beckett: A Collection of Critical Essays*. Englewood Cliffs, N.J.: Prentice - Hall, 1965.

____. *The Theatre of the Absurd*. New York: Doubleday, 1961.

Gottfried, Martin. *A Theater Divided*. Boston: Little, Brown, 1967. (Paperback edition, 1969)

Gregory, Horace. "Beckett's Dying Gladiators." *Commonweal*. October 26, 1956.

Hoffman, Frederick J. *Samuel Beckett: The Language of Self*. Carbondale, Illinois: Southern Illinois University Press, 1962. (Paperback edition, E. P. Dutton, 1964)

Johnson, Raymond. "Waiting for Beckett." *Adam*. Vol. 35, Nos. 337-339, 1970.

Kenner, Hugh. *Flaubert, Joyce and Beckett: The Stoic Comedians*. Boston: Beacon Press, 1962.

____. *Samuel Beckett: A Critical Study*. New York: Grove Press, 1961.

Kern, Edith. "Drama Stripped for Inaction: Beckett's *Godot*." *Yale French Studies*. No. 14, Winter 1954-1955.

Lahr, John. *Up against the Fourth Wall: Essays on Modern Theater*. New York: Grove Press, 1970.

Lumley, Frederick. *Trends in Twentieth Century Drama*. London: Barrie and Rockliff, 1960.

Manning, Hugo. "A Man to Remember." *Adam*. Vol. 35, Nos. 337-339, 1970.

McCoy, Charles S. "*Waiting for Godot*: A Biblical Appraisal." *Religion in Life*. Vol. XXVIII, Autumn 1959.

Rexroth, Kenneth. "The Point is Irrelevance." *The Nation*, April 14, 1956.

Robinson, Michael. *The Long Sonata of the Dead*. New York: Grove Press, 1970.

Saroyan, William. "A Few Words about Samuel Beckett's *Waiting for Godot.*" *Introduction to Columbia Masterworks Album* 02L-238.

Simpson, Alan. *Beckett and Behan and a Theatre in Dublin.* London: Routledge and Keagan Paul, 1962.

Tindall, William York. *Samuel Beckett.* Columbia University, 1964.

Wellwarth, George E. *The Theater of Protest and Paradox.* New York University Press, 1964.

www.ingramcontent.com/pod-product-compliance
Lightning Source LLC
LaVergne TN
LVHW011719060526
838200LV00051B/2955